Colorado Snow

And Other Humorous and Inspirational Stories

William J. Senn, III

William J. Senn, III

Luke 21:32

432/5508

All Scripture quotations are from the King James Version.

Previously called *Sermons with Too Much Tale*
First Edition: 20 Copies on December 10, 1992
Second Edition: 50 copies on December 17, 1992
Third Edition: 100 copies on December 19, 1997
Fourth Edition: 30 copies on December 18, 2001
Fifth Edition: 50 copies on December 25, 2003

Copyright 2009 by William J. Senn, III

All rights reserved

ISBN: 978-0-578-00929-2

COLORADO SNOW – First Edition: March 2009

Published by:
CROSS IMPACT PRESS
William J. Senn, III

6953 West 92nd Lane
Westminster, CO 80021
email: wsenn@tricitybaptist.org

Cover and interior design by Steven Plummer, Bethany Press International
Printed by Bethany Press International

Editor – Mary Vose
(Mary does not want her name "mentioned." To me "mention" has an audible ring to it. So, I will not "mention" it, but will only type it! Please do not "mention" that I cited her as my editor.)

PREFACE

COLORADO SNOW formerly called SERMONS WITH TOO MUCH TALE is dedicated to my precious wife, Allissa, as well as the church staff, deacons and members of University Baptist Church in Clemson, South Carolina. I am especially grateful for Mrs. Marge Brondyke who not only faithfully cleans the church with her husband Doug, but also has inspired and encouraged me to put down in writing my pulpit tales.

This book could have easily been given other titles such as: THE AUTOBIOG-RAPHY OF A YANKEE PREACHER, or TALL PREACHERS WITH TALL TALES, or ANOTHER CHAPTER TO MY BOOK, or LONG SERMONS AND SHORT STORIES, or HOW TO MAKE A LONG STORY LONGER, etc.

To the ear the word "tale" could also be understood to mean "tail" or, for our Southern friends, even "tell" could be a consideration in its conversational usage. With these three uses in mind, I have selected the word "TALE" for the title. The Senn family has been notorious for its incredible tales, from UFO sightings to an actual family photograph of an encounter of the second kind with the Loch Ness Monster. However, these TALES are almost all true stories, with only the names changed in some instances to protect the guilty. If you think some of these stories are too far-fetched, please keep in mind that each has been sanctified in the pulpit ministry at University Baptist Church or Tri-City Baptist Church, or otherwise they could not be used in SERMONS WITH TOO MUCH TALE.

SERMONS WITH TOO MUCH TALE could have been altered to SER-MONS WITH TOO MUCH TELL. I am extremely thankful for the patience of a church family who has persevered nine full years with my lengthy sermons, six of which were spent with them sitting on hard metal chairs.

This book could also have interchanged the word "TAIL" for "TALE" in its title due to the nature and intent of the book. The word "tail" quickly paints a picture in my mind of some animal's tail, particularly a dog's tail. However, for my purposes, I think of Charles Haddon Spurgeon's sermon illustration of the kite that had too much tail to get off the ground. His application of the kite with too much tail was that in many churches there are too many chiefs holding the string hence too much tail to get the work done or for the kite to ever fly. These stories may never get off the ground, because of too much "tail," "tale," and "tell," but I hope that they will be a blessing and an encouragement to you who read them. Since our family moved to Colorado in 2002, we have enjoyed the Rocky Mountains and Colorado snow. I have added several chapters to **SERMONS WITH TOO MUCH TALE** that have a Colorado flavor. Hence, the title change, **COLORADO SNOW**! I am hoping that this title has a wider appeal to the audience so that the Bible's narrow message would be read by more.

Soli Deo Gloria,
William J. Senn, III

TABLE OF CONTENTS

The chapter is about a scoundrel, but Skongal is not a misprint. Skongal was a character in my grandfather's book, *Mrs. Caliper's House*. Skongal was a light house operator and needed the light to be happy. I was a scoundrel and like Skongal was not satisfied until I received the Light.

"A MERRY HEART DOETH GOOD LIKE A MEDICINE."
PROVERBS 17:22

CHAPTER ONE

COLORADO SNOW

I am still amazed with all the snow showers we have been getting and then even more amazed as to how quickly the snow disappears. I have kept a journal of all the snow and our response to it since moving to Colorado from South Carolina on July 3, 2002. Hopefully, you will appreciate our growing appreciation for snow in Colorado.

July 4, 2002 – 6:00 p.m. We just arrived yesterday to our new church, Tri-City Baptist. It began snowing at 6:00 p.m. It was absolutely beautiful to see the snow mingled in with the fireworks. Allissa and I brewed some coffee and romantically looked out over the open space to watch the prairie dogs hide from the blanket of snow that was covering them. It looked like nature was tucking them into bed. I forgot how beautiful snow is. We felt so refreshed and rejuvenated. We both felt like teenagers again. I absolutely love snow.

July 9, 2002 – 7:00 a.m. We woke up this morning to a fresh coat of snow painted on our front yard. The snow sparkled when the sun hit it. Our sprinkling system was not needed and I turned it off to allow God's own beautiful system to work its nitrogenic wonders. We cannot imagine living in a lovelier place than in Denver, Colorado. I was counseled by Dave S. and Gary Oliver to buy a house with a southern exposure. This we did. We thought this was because they thought we might be homesick for the south. The real reason is that a driveway with a southern exposure would melt off the snow by noon. Despite this knowledge, I borrowed our neighbor's ergonomic shovel and went out to shovel the driveway and sidewalk just for the fun of it. It felt so good to get some exercise. I absolutely love snow.

July 15, 2002 – Noon. Last night's snow melted again by lunchtime. The mountains look absolutely spectacular. I hope that there will be snow in heaven. I realize that the New Jerusalem will rest upon a new earth that appears to be tropical in nature, but I would like to think there still will be snow somewhere. Each day in Colorado the mountains look different. Between the smoke from the fires and the snow on the peaks, I don't know what looks prettier. Both seem to serve as nature's smoke signals for man to reflect on God's creation. We took the Woosters to Estes Park and hiked around Bear Lake in the Rocky Mountain National Park. There were several glaciers in view with much snow. I absolutely love the snow. I can't wait for the next snow. I hope we have a white Christmas! It sure looks promising. I love snow.

July 21, 2002– We awoke to 9 inches of snow this morning. I quickly ran outside to see how my pink flamingos looked with snow up to their beaks. They are such beautiful birds and are rarely seen covered with snow. I saw our neighbor Bob shoveling his sidewalk. He asked what I thought of all the snow. I said, "I love snow!" He said by the end of the snow season in June that I would hate snow and be glad to have two weeks in the summer without it. I told him that would be quite impossible for, "I love snow."

I really like Bob; he is a great neighbor, although I hardly see him. One thing I like about Bob is that he allowed his garage door to stay up for over five minutes one time. This truly shows a unique openness. Since my office is facing the street, I can see everyone drive in and out of our neighborhood. I actually keep a pad on my desk to time how long the garage door stays open for each of our neighbors. Steve, I have noticed is the fastest. His door never stays open for more than three seconds. He almost hits the door as he drives in and pulls right up to a dangling tennis ball suspended from the ceiling of the garage on a string (very clever!). His timing however is impeccable and he seems to have a knack of just missing the door. Mrs. Linda Nelson is the standard-bearer for openness in the neighborhood with her door staying open for an average of forty-four seconds!

We have a HOA policy (#3268a) that states if you see anyone's garage door open for more than fifteen minutes, the neighborly thing to do is to tell your neighbor. We have already met one neighbor who came by to tell us that our garage door was open. It was 9:00 p.m. and it had been open probably since before dinner. One thing I have noticed is that several neighbors have in their garage a snow-blower, a plow or a handful of shovels. I am still not sure why. All I know is that I absolutely love snow!

August 2, 2002 – It snowed again last night, but disappeared by noon. When I went out to get the mail, I actually saw a neighbor out of his house and expressed my disappointment that the snow was all gone. He said that by the end of the season we would be terribly sick of snow and that it might even drive me to the funny farm. I told him that could not be possible. I love snow.

August 9, 2002 – Boys had football camp in the snow. I sat in the truck and watched the snow accumulate to 4 inches. It is absolutely freezing outside. I was told by one of the coaches that this was nothing; that they had played in weather where the footballs lost all air pressure due to the cold and that they had to play with a flat-pigskin in snow drifts up to 8 feet high. He also mentioned something about not being able to drive over the passes in such weather. I have heard of the forward pass, lateral pass, but never "drive over the pass." I just nodded my head, so I wouldn't look dumb. I am still confused about the pass being closed due to snow. Apparently, in snowstorms you must rely on the running game solely. My rear-wheel drive truck slipped and slid all the way home from Longmont in the snow. I am planning to trade in the truck for a 4x4 Ford Exploder or a Jeep Arapaho if it continues to snow through the fall. I love driving in snow.

August 23, 2002 – First day of school. We thought for sure school would be canceled due to the 9 inches of snowfall last night. The Yurkas kept their kids home from school and so did we. We assumed school was canceled, but heard later that Faith Baptist never closes school for a snowstorm. Hopefully, we can get the kids to school tomorrow.

Allissa thinks we should probably buy the boys some winter coats. Burlington Coat Factory has a sale going on so we will probably break down and get them some coats. We have not had to purchase winter coats for twenty-one years. For some reason, I think we are going to need them out here.

Everyone at church keeps asking us how we like the weather. We were told that Denver had 300 days of blue skies. Apparently, that means even if there was only 30 seconds of blue sky somewhere over the Columbine state that this would count as one of the 300 days. What I think they meant was that there will be 300 days of snow showers each year. People like to use the words: "precipitation" or "moisture" a lot. I think in terms of rain, snow, sleet, etc. Regardless, my general answer to folks is that we love snow.

September 1, 2002 – They are forecasting 14 inches for tomorrow. Sold my truck and bought a 4x4. Also I bought snow tires for my wife's minivan, the boys' bicycles, and chains for the widow maker (my Honda 750 motorcycle). Just in time too. The wind is really blowing hard today. We keep losing shingles from such blasts. I now understand why the previous owner left behind the bundles of shingles, but why thirty-seven bundles?

I forgot to drain the water from the pipes of watering/irrigation system. I noticed a steady stream of water motoring into our neighbor's yard. This is obviously a major HOA grievance (#5822b). Did shut off all water once I figured out where the main was. Rick Schrecengost came by to blow out all the water from the pipes which were not broken. The force from his huge compressor was so great that he blew aspen leaves back up the pipes into all the commodes. What a mess!

Dick Vose later came by and spent three hours meticulously duct-taping pipes which he had surrounded with insulation with an R-250 rating. He spent one-hour teaching me how to operate our sprinkling system and two hours explaining the diagram on the back of the box. Due to the Denver climate and the drought, the Bluebird watering system can only be used sparingly in the "summer." Snow began to fall. I love snow.

September 2, 2002 – Wow what a snow! Unfortunately, the electricity went out. I did not sleep well last night. Some idiot woke us up at 3:00 a.m. by firing up his snow-blower. Apparently, he wanted to keep pace with the snowstorm. I don't mean to call him an idiot, but it wasn't very thoughtful for him to wake us up. He is an interesting guy. He goes out every hour on the hour and blows his driveway and sidewalks off. I learned that it is a HOA mandate (#33331c) that each house owner is responsible for clearing his own driveway and sidewalk within thirty minutes of the first sign of snow. It looks like I am going to have to buy a shovel after all.

The boys want me to buy a four-wheeler, in particular what I think they call a Honda George Foreman, with a snowplow in the front. They said they could make thousands of dollars plowing snow for people in the neighborhood. The snow was very light, but it still took considerable time to shovel with my spade and hole digger. The boys were not around to help. I really need one of those ergonomic shovels. The house was without electricity for most of the day. Allissa thinks we should buy a wood stove.

September 3, 2002 – Some snow melted, but turned into ice. As I walked outside this morning to fetch the newspaper, I slipped on the ice. There was no warning and then all of a sudden the *Denver Post* was flying in all directions. My how I hurt like the dickens. I love snow, but I do not like the ice.

October 31, 2002 – I have been joking at church weekly about all the blizzards that we have been having. They keep telling me that I ain't seen nothing yet. Today it snowed 18 inches. Sure looks like a blizzard. After shoveling the sidewalk, the snowplow came through our neighborhood and sprayed 3 feet of snow back on my sidewalk. Idiot! The kids are no where to be seen to help with the shoveling. They are out with their friends sledding and having a snowball fight. Allissa and I have been home fighting. She wants a wood stove. I told her that we would hardly use it and that there is no firewood in the Denver area anyway since there are no trees. Certainly, the people in the People's Republic of Boulder would agree that man should not use trees for heating purposes, only couches.

November 2, 2002 – The wind last night was unbelievable. I thought the house was going to blow away. We lost a bunch of shingles and the wind blew over our grill and our playground equipment. Allissa wants me to sell the playground equipment so we can purchase a wood stove. The boys are still pitching me for a four-wheeler. Electricity did come back on after dinner. Truly amazing that Papa Johns delivers in this kind of weather.

November 5, 2002 – Warmed up to four degrees today. It is the first day in over a month that the temperature was above zero. Allissa thinks that we should buy winter coats. I finally agreed. We purchased two matching Columbia ski coats. They really look cool, but are actually quite warm. We also purchased a family ski package which included three rentals, three lessons, an autographed poster of Dr. Olson snow-boarding at 95 mph over a 1,000-foot precipice and an unlimited ski pass for Keystone, Breckenridge and A-Basin. I can't wait for Frank Johnson to join us at Thanksgiving. We are going to take him with us skiing. Like our boys, he wants to learn how to snowboard.

November 26, 2002 – Frank Johnson arrived. We had a great Thanksgiving dinner. Tomorrow we are planning to go skiing. We have been told two ways to get to Keystone. One is through the Eisenhower Tunnel and the other route is over the Loveland Pass. We now know what a pass is. Allissa is a little nervous about skiing.

November 27, 2002 – We went through the Tunnel. As we came out on the other side, we drove right into what I would call a blizzard. This seemed impossible for on one side of the Tunnel was blue skies and bighorn sheep grazing on the side of the road. On the other side of the Tunnel, there was no light, snow coming at us in a rage, and truckers on the side of the road wrapping their tires in chains.

We slowed down to a snail's pace as we inched down the 6 miles of mountain. We also had seen earlier the results of a real avalanche. It never connected until I saw the massive pile-up of trees at the base of the mountain that we really live in Avalanche country. It would not surprise me some day to see someone out here call their favorite sports team, the Avalanche.

With the heavy snow conditions, Allissa now was on avalanche alert. She had the boys looking out their windows to catch the first glimpse of any impending avalanches. The boys thought she was being ridiculous, but then Allissa saw a sign by the side of the road that said, "Avalanche Area." When the boys read that sign, they began to take their duty of looking for avalanches quite seriously.

I was trying to watch the road which seemed to have disappeared because of the snow. I love snow. However, I am not too excited about snow when I can't see the road in front of me. We were passed by every car and 18-wheeler on the highway. I have been told by westerners that I drive like a South Carolinian or a flatlander in the mountains, whatever that means. Allissa was also worried about us sliding off the edge down one of the banks. Somehow and someway we made it to Keystone.

We all put on our snow clothes and ski boots and began the trek to our first ski lesson. We got lost and just missed the early ski lesson we had left so early in the morning to make (4:30 a.m.). Frank said he didn't need any lessons to snowboard. He is a big skateboarder, so off he went. Later, we would find him walking down the slopes with snowboard in tow and with a bloody nose. The snow was beautiful on the slopes.

Our lessons were helpful despite Allissa skiing off the top of the mountain and landing upside down in the tree line. She said she was run off the slope by some out of control snowboarder which she thought looked a lot like Frank. The boys did not master the snowboard either and were very disappointed. I had a blast and did not taste the snow once all day. The lesson was helpful for me and gave me great hope that some day I would be able to turn right on the slopes.

As we drove home, we were all exhausted, a little grumpy and a lot hungry. We had only eaten one million-dollar pizza at the lodge on the summit where each pepperoni slice added to the pizza was fifteen dollars. We learned quickly that the next time we would bring our own food. Overall, it was a great day, and we saw a lot of snow.

December 24, 2002 – We are dreaming of a white Christmas, but I don't think it is going to happen. It is eighty-four degrees outside and blue skies. It has snowed almost every day since we moved here, but not now. I hope the kids won't be disappointed. I can't wait for Christmas tomorrow. I bought Allissa a wood stove. Last year I bought her a vacuum cleaner and for some reason she did not like it as a Christmas gift. Hopefully, she will respond to the wood stove more warmly. I even found a dead tree in Golden to split for firewood. Of course, the firewood would be part of the Christmas gift. I do not want to leave anything undone. I actually put a red bow on the kindling wood.

For the boys' major Christmas gift I have purchased three ergonomic snow shovels. I had Debbie Robbins write each of the boy's names in calligraphy on the shovel heads. I had seen her work on saws and spoons and thought what a great idea for shovels. The boys I thought would love it and what a great way to keep their shovels ergonomically straight as to the rightful owner. We had a great Christmas Eve service at church. People keep asking me how I like the weather. I do love snow.

Christmas Day – NO snow, oh no! Allissa was so surprised about the wood stove that she was speechless. It must have overwhelmed her because she has not said a word to me all day. The boys thought the shovels were stupid. My gifts that I opened included pink flamingo salt and pepper shakers, pink flamingo slippers, a pink flamingo pen set, pink flamingo stationery, a pink flamingo tie, pink flamingo underwear, pink flamingo dice for the 4x4, pink flamingo mittens and a pink flamingo doorstop. I will stop there. Needless to say, our first Christmas in Denver was more a pink Christmas than a white Christmas.

December 26, 2002 – For the first time in our family's history, our whole family flew together on Pink Flamingo Airlines to Detroit and then to Elmira, New York to celebrate the holiday season with Allissa's and my family. What a great time we had. They had a white Christmas. We enjoyed a whole week of snow. Most memorable was my hike with the boys up to Austinville and over the hill back to grandmother's house hunting for deer. It was truly a winter wonderland. I love snow.

January 15, 2003 – We kept the kids home from school today. Despite the 90-mph winds, the ice storm, 2 feet of snow, and the presence of the National Guard, Faith Baptist School remained open today. We were not going to take the chance to drive up to school today. The Yurkas stayed home. Chris Scheetz however drove her kids to school despite the inclement weather. The kids say she sings opera music all the way to Longmont and is able to tune out all obstacles. Due to the poor weather it took her an abnormally long time, about fifteen minutes, to go the thirty-one miles to Faith. I am glad she made it safely to school, but we still felt we made the right decision to keep our kids at home.

This really feels like a blizzard today. It has snowed now fourteen of the fifteen days in 2003. We watched "It's a Wonderful Life" three times today. I shoveled the drive twice today. Thought I was going to have a heart attack. Very tired and a little grumpy and wish the snow would hurry up and melt. Allissa is very tired of all the mess in the house. The kids keep tracking in a lot of snow and every time I walk in the kitchen or laundry room in my socks I get wet feet.

I burned a nice pair of wool socks on the wood stove while trying to dry them. The flames set off the smoke alarms in the house. I ripped all batteries out of fire alarms. The kids must have changed clothes six times today. The garage has puddles of water in it. I don't know why they didn't slope the concrete in the garage away from the house rather than into the house.

January 16, 2003 – Snowed again. Pipes froze. The electricity is off. Glad we have the wood stove but should have listened to Allissa and split some more firewood. We are out of wood. We cut the handles off the $39.95 ergonomic shovels to keep the fire going. I stayed warm for a while. Kids home again from school. They are driving us a little crazy. Clothes hanging in garage to dry but froze instead.

January 17, 2003 – Snowed again. It warmed up to –35. The snowplow went by and sprayed 2 feet of snow on our freshly shoveled driveway. Have you ever shoveled snow with ergonomic shovels without handles? Hardly ergonomical! Bob, our neighbor asked how I liked the snow. I didn't really want to answer him. I forced a smile.

March 18, 2003 – Today will go down as the Blizzard of 2003. I received 2,189 emails today and 3,901 phone calls. They all had one message in common. This is a blizzard! I have never seen so much snow in all my life. Several people told me to shovel the snow off the roof or it could possibly cave in. Allissa did not want me on the roof. I told her that I would be just fine, but she raised the roof with her concerns about me falling off and how she could not get me to the hospital because of the roads. I would not admit it, but she was probably right. The boys built an igloo outside in the front yard.

March 19, 2003 – The boys slept in the igloo last night. While they slept, we froze. The electricity went off. Wood stove out of wood again. I should have listened to my wife. We used puzzles as kindling wood, but needed something more substantial to keep the fire going. Allissa said we should pray about it. So I did. Later that day the roof caved in. A mixed blessing, but clearly an answer to prayer in that we were able to use the damaged 2x4's as firewood.

It was a long day to say the least. We were able to stretch plastic over the roof, but the wind kept blowing it off. We were able finally to duct-tape the plastic sheet down by using the boy's bicycles as anchor weights in the corners. It really was quite clever if you could see it. Today, we were fined by the HOA (#33331c) for not shoveling the 4 feet of snow off our sidewalks within the thirty-minute time period. There will be an additional fifty-dollar fine for each half-hour that the sidewalks remain not shoveled. The boys were not here to help shovel, but went to church for a big snowball fight. The snow was so heavy! My back is killing me! I got "a little grumpy" with Allissa when she asked if I was going to shovel off the back porch to make a path to the bird feeder so she could feed the birds.

March 20, 2003 – Unexpectedly, Allissa went home to her mother's today. She left on United, but the note she left behind could have been entitled Divided.

April 20, 2003 – Easter. Allissa just returned from her mothers. She has been gone a month. Great to have Allissa back for the holiday. It snowed yesterday in the foothills, absolutely beautiful morning.

April 25, 2003 – I finally yielded to Allissa's plea to see a doctor. The fact that she said she would take the kids back with her to momma had nothing to do with me making the appointment. I met with Dr. Phil Orpah Freud. He believes what I need is some rest. He gave me white, snow-like pills, but I overreacted. Then I was fitted in a nice white jacket. The doctor's diagnosis is that I simply have been snowed under.

I hate snow!

COLORADO SNOW is mostly original, but the general idea came from the "Banana Belt Diary" and the adaptation that Lonnie Schmid sent me from Mikey's Funnies. For you who are still wondering about the accuracy of all the snow excerpts and dates it is important that you know that I have taken some literary license in the journal, COLORADO SNOW. This chapter is dedicated to Gary and Jackie Oliver who worked so hard in getting us out to Colorado. Also, one clarification if needed is that I love Colorado snow!

CHAPTER TWO

THE DAY THE YOKE WAS ON ME

I couldn't wait! It was the last day of school in Pennsylvania. I had survived another school year, this time eighth grade. I had counted down the days for school to end and for summer to begin, which unofficially was reckoned by the last day of school. I rose early in the morning and pondered my game plan for making the biggest splash possible at the sock hop. Most of my friends had purchased water guns or balloons to be modified into exploding blimps for the after-school activities. That was fine for them, but just didn't seem challenging enough to me; besides last year I was loaded for bear with water guns, which backfired on me because of the leaks in the guns. I had been somewhat embarrassed by the guns because of the watermarks they left on my trousers as I tried to conceal the deadly arsenal in my pockets. Someone still needs to invent a water gun that doesn't leak around the plug.

As I meditated on what I should bring to school my mother asked if I wanted French toast, my favorite, for breakfast. This would be a real treat compared to the daily pre-school consumption of Carnation's Instant Breakfast and Pop-Tarts. When my mother cracked the eggs for the French toast, the idea hit me. Why not bring several eggs to school and use them in the fight after school or even in a bombing raid on the bus on the way home? I had perfect peace that my plans would not be scrambled, so I slyly removed two eggs from the carton and placed them in the pocket of my mother's blue nylon jacket, which was somewhat too big for me.

After eating breakfast, I waited in the kitchen listening for Bus #4 to come roaring down to the bridge on Dowlin Forge Road. Once the bus crossed the bridge, I could easily walk down the side steps to the road and wait for it to stop in front of our house. I was the only one Mrs. Lockard picked up at this stop on the country route that specialized in transporting country bumpkins. After saying good-bye to Mom, I ran out to get on the bus, being very careful that my two bombs were not bumped and that I did not sit on them. After some close calls I sat down and off we rattled up the serpentine hill to pick up the Moores, Harlow Melton, and the Nothstines.

We arrived at school in time for all the festivities of the last half-day of school. After homeroom and the returning and stacking of books, our class had snacks and refreshments. My friends thought it odd that I was wearing a jacket on this warm June day, but I dismissed their curiosity by saying I had caught a summer cold.

Following our classroom party, the entire Lionville Junior High School, which consisted of grades seven through nine, was brought into the main auditorium for a sock hop. What luck! I hadn't worn socks that day due to the high likelihood of much man-made precipitation. Consequently I was not prepared to dance and felt quite safe.

The music started blaring over the speakers and a few students made their way to the platform to dance. There was just something unappealing about dancing in front of the whole school at 11:00 a.m. Besides, most of the crowd dancing was girls dancing with girls, with just a smattering of some cootsie-wootsie boys. You wouldn't catch me dead up there dancing.

Then the fast-paced music changed into a slow dance. To my surprise, Karen MacDonald asked me to dance. I had had a crush on her for two years and had sadly watched my puppy love go to the dogs. (I could still remember her braces sparkling in the lights at the seventh grade dance when I danced with her.) After stuttering I said, "Sure."

As we walked up the stairs to the platform it was like walking the stairway to heaven, but then it hit me that I better beat it quick because in my pocket were two time bombs that would certainly be detonated in a slow dance. This was terrible, what a predicament! How could I turn her down now? I couldn't be chicken! Too late, oomph, she grabbed me and started dancing! She must have thought I had cracked judging by the expression on her face.

She knew I liked her because I had written her love letters all year in Biology class and signed them Marvin. Marvin, who was quite heavy, had the facial marks of an eighth grader in transition, and hair that could have been used as an alternate oil source during the oil embargo, told Karen the letters were from me.

During the second rotation of our dance, I knew the eggs in my jacket would either hatch or break. The inevitable happened and the dance was over-easy, even before the song ended. I could feel the slime filling my pocket and permeating the perforations in the nylon jacket. I could see my horrified face reflected in Karen's braces, so I quickly said to her that I didn't feel well and needed to run to the bathroom. Off I ran, leaving a soupy trail behind me. I still don't understand why she never wanted to dance with me again after that day.

There was only a little sand left in my egg timer before school would be let out and I would be exposed as the one who had made the dance floor hazardous. Two of my classmates had just been paddled by Mr. Stoner, the principal, for their destructive behavior at the dance. Would I be next? Would I be classified as a bad egg by the administration? Would my perfect record be smeared? I felt fried!

Finally the bell rang and the egg dilemma was over-easy, or so I thought. The students were dismissed to go to their busses. I sneaked out of the bathroom and made a mad dash to bus #4 before I could be traced. Was I ever relieved to get on the bus and sit down in my favorite seat over the rear wheel well on the left side of the bus by the window! As the bus pulled off, I watched with some amusement, the expressions on the faces of the teachers and the principal as they guided the buses out of the parking lot. It almost looked like they were glad to see the kids go!

The bus was noisier than ever. Kids were screaming and throwing water balloons and squirting each other with their previously concealed water guns. We could see Mrs. Lockard's troubled face in her mirror - the mirror that gave her eyes in the back of her head. She was a very capable bus driver and could easily muscle the big, yellow, submarine down the road. She was one woman I wouldn't want to mess with! After almost everyone's ammunition was exhausted, I began to think of the one remaining egg in my jacket that had not broken at the dance. I know I should have thrown it away at school in the bathroom, but, for one reason or another, I just didn't.

On the bus was Harlow Melton. I had chummed around with him for awhile, but we had drifted apart because of a lack of common interests. Harlow had patterned his dress and hairstyle after some passing rock group called the Beatles.

He had gone hog wild after them which had bugged me. In fact, he let his hair grow over his ears and almost down to his collar. He also wore bell-bottom pants, which looked kind of funny. Who would ever wear those? I had always dismissed his oddities and his funny British accent because he had not yet fully adjusted to the American lifestyle since moving over with his family from England.

Harlow was sitting in the front of the bus on the fourth row. My mind began to wander thinking how funny it would be to hit Harlow on the top of his shaggy rug. The more I thought of it, the more convinced I became that I needed to make the launch. It was going to be a tough shot but, being a dead-eye pitcher, I knew I could hit the mark. The tricky part would be throwing it so no one would know where it came from. It only took a few additional moments to build up my courage before Harlow's bus stop. Finally, the moment arrived. I cocked my arm and let her fly straight towards Harlow in perfect hand-grenade form. Close doesn't count except in horseshoes, hand-grenades and egg tosses. To my horror, the egg went right over the top of Harlow's mop and squarely hit the head of Janet Nothstine's little sister, Dorcas. Dorcas was a sweet little girl who always quietly rode the bus home. That would all change. This time she let out a high-pitched scream at ground zero and continued to cry as she swept the yolk and shells out of her pretty hair. Well, scratch ever taking Janet Nothstine out!

Immediately Mrs. Lockard slammed on the brakes and pulled the bus off the side of the road in front of the McGuigin's house. She first looked at Dorcas and tried to console her by assuring her she would find the culprit. She waddled towards the back of the bus and demanded that the person who had thrown the egg stand up. I could feel my face turning ten shades of rooster red. In these situations, my face would turn red and I would look and feel guilty, even if I was perfectly innocent. This time I was guilty. All I could hope was that no one had seen me throw the egg or, if they had, that they would not squeal. Mrs. Lockard then said, "If no one is going to admit it, I will turn this bus around and return to the school. We will stay there until the principal finds out whodunit." Now what? Do I admit it, or bring the whole bus back to school for an unscheduled Easter egg hunt, which no one wanted to do? I sat quietly but could not bring myself to own up to my disgraceful act.

Finally, after what seemed like an eternity, Mrs. Lockard made her way back to the front and continued on her route. Was I ever glad when my stop finally came! I sheepishly said, "Goodbye Mrs. Lockard. I'll see you next school year," and ran off to my house. For some reason I could not enjoy the special lunch and treats that Mom had prepared for our celebration of the last day of school. I felt so bad inside.

Mom thought I was just feeling empty, anticipating a summer of missing the constant interaction with my friends at school.

Summer flew by! Wearing my new sneakers, I stood by the kitchen door listening for Bus #4 to downshift before reaching the bridge. This year Randie, my brother, would be in seventh grade and I would be in ninth. We would ride the bus together to Lionville Junior High. The next year I would go into the tenth grade and take a different bus to Downingtown Senior High School. We both waved good bye to Mom. It almost looked like she was glad to see us go. In fact, her look was reminiscent of the teachers' looks when the students had left for summer vacation.

Mrs. Lockard greeted both Randie and me kindly as we got onto the bus. The bus was crowded with only a few aisle seats left, which would make for an uncomfortable 5 miles to school. I was glad that I did not have to ride the bus home each night, since I played on the football, basketball and baseball teams after school. My bus driver in the evenings would be my mother. She would graciously take home all the stray kids who needed rides after practice regardless of how "on-the-way" or "close" they lived.

Ninth grade seemed to float by with its many ups and downs. This year on the last day of school, I was feeling quite empty as I glared out the windows into the valley before me. In the glass, I could physically see a reflection. Likewise, mentally, I could see pictures and reflections of the friends and fun that I had had during my three years of Junior High. I sadly knew I would never routinely walk the halls of Lionville Junior High again. I regretted the thoughts that I would never again play competitively on the fields as a Lion. I looked backwards, I looked forwards, and then I just looked. It was time to go, to step forward and to leave behind the place I loved.

The bell rang! The students were buzzing about and, like cows being called in from the fields lined themselves up in front of their respective six-wheel, moving stalls. During homeroom for the past week, it had been announced that there would be no water guns permitted on any of the buses and that anyone found with H_2O bombs, eggs, etc. would be suspended. That did not affect my plans because I was in an introspective mood, splashing in the events of my life. It was agonizing to let go of what had been a special part of my life for three years.

On the ride home, the bus seemed to be on tracks and was moving rapidly towards its many destinations down the windy, bumpy, country road. I hardly noticed that Mrs. Lockard had stopped in front of the McGuigin's house, which was unusual since there were no kids there and consequently, no need of a bus stop.

I was staring out the window from my favorite seat over the rear wheels. That was the best ride on the bus, especially when Mrs. Lockard hit the speed bumps at school. Mrs. Lockard had stopped the bus and was now waddling down the aisle. The bus was noisy and I figured she had seen someone really misbehaving in the back seats and in need of a real good tongue-lashing. She quietly walked past my seat and I lost sight of her from my peripheral vision. It was then that Mrs. Lockard's incubator, which had been heating up for 365 days, was opened.

To my surprise, I heard a crack and felt the gushy sensation of egg yolk dripping down from my long hair onto my face and onto my bell-bottoms. The kids on the bus howled. Even Dorcas Nothstine laughed, which I thought was only kosher. Mrs. Lockard said she had looked forward to doing this to me for one whole year. What I had totally forgotten, she had not. I don't know how she kept it in all year without letting me know she was aware of my last-day shenanigans, but she did. I was humiliated, but, being a good sport, could only laugh with her and the rest of the kids. Breakfast, I mean, justice had been served!

When I got off the bus, I knew this would be my last ride with Mrs. Lockard. We grinned at each other and laughed as I thanked her for being my bus driver. Then I told her, "I will get you back for this raw deal, but for now THE YOLK'S ON ME!"

THIS CHAPTER IS DEDICATED to all my former teachers and school bus drivers while in public school. You were a brave lot! I am especially thankful for Mr. Wolf, Mr. Randy Epler, Coach Wright, Coach Joe and Mrs. Carrol Kreider and for the fond and not so fond memories at Mary C. House, Exton Elementary, Lionville Elementary, Downingtown Middle School - 6th Grade, Lionville Jr. High, Downingtown Sr. High and Twin Valley Sr. High Schools.

CHAPTER THREE

THE GREAT PUMPKIN RIDE

It was a cold November day in the year 1978, when as a sophomore in college; I decided on the spur of the moment to pack my bags and head home for the weekend to see first my father and then my mother. I threw into the back of my 65 VW bug my dirty laundry. Oddly, all my whites had uniformly turned out to be pink after my first attempt of doing laundry at college. I really don't know what happened, for I had never experienced this problem before during my freshman year; then again I couldn't remember if I had ever washed my clothes that year. Anyway, certainly mom could remedy the problem with the pinks. It was only 50 miles to my father's house from Elizabethtown College. The hour drive went quickly as I sailed east down the leafless corridor of Route 30.

My father and my stepmother Lynn were surprised to see me when I pulled in. We enjoyed just getting caught up with all the news regarding the family as well as all my stories about college life. I told dad how much I had missed riding a motorcycle while away at school and that I was itching just to go for a short ride on one of his motorcycles. I knew that there was no chance that he would let me ride his 900cc Honda, and after previously wiping out and breaking Lynn's mirrors on her 350cc Yamaha, after a ride of only 20 feet, that there would not be much hope to ride hers either. So I asked if I could ride the 175 Yamaha which I used to ride before dad purchased me a 125 Hodaka Wombat. The Yamaha 175 was an on/off road bike, which dad had licensed for the road after I turned it over to him when I crashed it into a telephone pole.

I could still vividly remember that crash and burn. I was riding a wheelie through the field, which was across from our old house, when the rear tire suddenly pivoted. With the front wheel up in the air, it was hard to steer the bike away from the telephone pole that stood firmly in front of me.

I could have called for help, but the line I was on was too busy to dial 911. All I could remember was the loud CRASH! The next thing I knew I was rolling in the road wondering if I was dead or if I just had a wrong number. Regardless my bell was rung!

The impact was so loud that my father ran out of the house instantly and could for a brief moment still see the telephone pole wavering. He ran across the street and immediately picked up the motorcycle to see if it was OK. It wasn't, both forks were bent at right angles back towards the engine. I thought, while still groaning and rolling on the side of the road, that if I could stand on my two forks that I would soon have another real shock to absorb. He was not too pleased with his oldest son's Evil Knievel imitation! Dad called immediately the motorcycle hospital and told them that his son had just hit a telephone pole and that the two front forks were bent on the bike. He then asked what it would cost to have them fixed. They oddly asked first, "Where should we send the flowers?" I think Dad thought they meant for the bike, but I think their question was directed towards me. I guess they thought that when one hits a telephone pole that there is usually a long distance call involved. Fortunately for me I was on call waiting at the time. With this background in mind, you can see why dad might hesitate in permitting me to take even a short trip on any of his bikes.

After the art of skilful persuasion was engaged, basically begging, dad reservedly said he would allow me to take one spin on the 175 Yamaha, but only around the block. The block was less than a mile in total distance. Could I be content with just 1 mile of riding? My dad did have a good point that I shouldn't be out on the major highways since I did not currently have an up-to-date-motorcycle-driving license.

To get a motorcycle out of one of dad's storage sheds is like taking a wedge of gold out of Fort Knox, definitely a maximum-security operation. I think dad has a key ring with keys to open his key ring, which has keys to open up the locks on the sheds, which has keys to unlock the chains on his bikes. Dad meticulously has each bike covered with a bed sheet which would be the envy of any of the guys on my hall back in the dorms. After all the maximum-security checkpoints were made it was then time for the unveiling. Dad then took further precaution to see if the bike was in perfect running order. I was afraid he was going to change the air in the tires, and further delay my escape on the Yamaha. I don't think he realized I had classes on Monday.

After what seemed like Fall Break, the bike was finally out of the shed and idling evenly. Of course, dad had to give me some last minute advice to take it easy as well as to come right back. I think he forgot that I had raced moto-cross in Pennsylvania's District 6, and that I was a very competent rider.

After putting on the Bell helmet with its abbreviated duckbill, I straddled old Yammie, engaged the clutch, and pressed the gearshift down one notch. I knew if I released the clutch too soon and started right off with a wheelie that Dad would pop a gasket. So I gently pulled out of the drive and up shifted smoothly through the next two gears before I hit the stop sign. Stop signs have a little more give in them than telephone poles.

It felt great to be back on a bike. It had been a good while since I had ridden. My Hodaka had died suddenly when I busted the main frame under the tank by jumping off the dam at Marsh Creek. My moto-cross bike, a Yamaha 125 YZ was ZZ after its tranny was shot with one too many speed shifts. So without a bike working for two years I was going through withdrawal symptoms, and today was just what the doctor had ordered.

After I made the first turn around the block, the handlebars took a funny turn left rather than right to continue the orbit around the block. It was almost like the bike had a mind of its own, which I could only surmise came from the eighteen horses that were hitched to its rear sprocket. You know how horses can be. It wasn't long before I was on the by-pass of Route 30 shifting from fourth to fifth and watching the tachometer redline. My eyes were watering and my hands were freezing so I backed off the throttle and leveled it off for the ride eastbound. I still didn't know where the bike was taking me, but it was very clear it wasn't around the block! All I could do was to hang on for dear life.

It didn't take me too long to see that old Yammie was somewhat homesick and wanted to see the old farmette on Dowlin Forge Road where it had spent most of its days getting broken in. I could tell old Yammie had been feeling somewhat cooped up in that shed and that he had been somewhat intimidated with big Daddy-O Honda strutting all of his 900cc. So what if Honda had four carburetors and four exhaust pipes and had a top-end of about 150-MPH! I tried to keep it all in perspective for Yammie and he kind of blew off some smoke giggling when I told him that old Honda couldn't go 1 mile with him over the trails and streams in the old valley. Honda was an asphalt hog, but Yammie could go anywhere! I also firmly reminded him that he had to have respect for all of his bigger Japanese ancestors.

Finally, in sight was our old house and red barn. I could tell, Yammie missed the old barn where he could kick back on his kick-stand and enjoy his old girl friend, a yellow Kawasaki. Between the two of them was parked junior, a little Honda 50. We slowly glided by the barn and then old Yammie swerved to the left as we passed the infamous telephone pole on the right. You could tell he had a real aversion for that pole. We glanced at the old house and the steps we used to ride up to get to the patio. We also saw the old trail that we blazed behind the house that went to the top of the mountain ridge. We were to use that trail to avoid the need of riding our dirt bikes on the road without a license. We both were sort of in low gear as we thought of all the wonderful times we shared in the forge.

Well, we didn't want to get bogged down, so I hit the old throttle and felt the surge to move on, especially with the haunting thought that my dad was probably still standing outside his shed waiting for his son's arrival. My fear was that the bike would go back permanently in the shed and that I might end up behind the shed.

We passed Becker's pond, and then leaned into the turn around Blindman's Bend. We then surfaced and were about to cross the bridge over the Shamona Creek, when I saw my old friend Slow Joe playing basketball in the driveway at his grandfather's. I was somewhat hesitant about stopping because I had deliberately distanced myself from Joe since we had moved out of the area some three years ago, but I felt an obligation to say hi to him. We had played many a game of hoops at his grandfather's where Joe had spent most of his childhood. I pulled up the drive and parked the bike. Joe knew immediately who it was when he heard and saw the bike, for we had ridden many times together when he had his Honda SL125. His Honda had taken the big jump after its last big whoopty-do and was laid down to rust in its berm.

Joe was glad to see me. We small talked as we shot baskets together. It was good to see him in some ways, but I knew that whenever we got together we inevitably would get in trouble. After getting a drink of water and saying hi to his grandparents, I told Joe that I needed to get back to my dad's. Joe immediately piped up and said, "You know I haven't seen your old man for awhile, how about me riding back with you to see him?" I replied, "I'm already in trouble Joe and I hate to drag you into what could be a very unpleasant scene since I have been gone already two hours, and besides how would you get there?" I shouldn't have asked that question, for I knew immediately I had left the door wide open. Joe kept on prying. He always had an uncommon way of maneuvering me to do things against my conscience and better judgment. He said, "I don't care, I think I can help you get out of this mess. He will be so happy to see me, that he won't say anything to you."

Well, perhaps he had a point. Joe could run some major interference for me and perhaps even have a calming effect on the entire situation. I then asked, "Joe, how do you plan to see my dad since you just totaled another car?" He immediately responded that he would ride on the back of the motorcycle. Well that did not interest me, because Dad never really liked us boys giving rides to anyone, but again that was his opinion three years ago. Certainly things have changed, especially since I was now a responsible college student fighting to keep my GPA above sea level. I said, "OK Joe, I will take you, but you will need to get your old green helmet since I did not bring another helmet."

At that time Pennsylvania had some of the strictest laws regarding transportation and some of the most severe fines in all the Union. They were very adamant in seeing motorcyclists wear their mandated helmets. Even the gangs, such as the Hell's Angels and the Warlocks wore makeshift helmets, and occasionally respected these laws. I was not opposed to the helmet law ever since a close friend of mine in high school lost her sister when she fell off the back of a motorcycle. She was not wearing a helmet when she landed on her head and died in the Downingtown High School parking lot. Can you imagine any state not having such an appropriate law as a mandatory helmet law?

Joe said he had sold his helmet to the men who picked up the remains of his Honda SL 125. Well I was somewhat relieved to hear that, because not only would it be a long ride with him on the back of the motorcycle, but it necessitated me going another hour out of my way to drop Joe back off before I went to my mother's for the night. He said he would go anyway without a helmet. I said, "No way, we would be picked up by the police for sure, and I don't want to do anything that would attract any attention to me anyway since I don't have a motorcycle driver's license and the bike itself does not have a current inspection sticker."

It was at that moment that Joe's and my eyes arrived at the same point. In the living room in the big picture window was a big, orange pumpkin that was set out as a decoration for Halloween. We both read each other's minds. Would it fit? It didn't take Joe long to carve out the pumpkin so that he could put his head in it. I tried not to laugh with all the slop and slime running down his bleached blond hair. We howled as he continued his humorous carvings. It was a very tight fit, but after cutting out holes for his nose, mouth and eyes, it truly looked quite convincing as an authentic, pumpkin-head helmet. We smiled with success, knowing once again that where there was a Joe and a Will, there was a way. If I stayed off the main roads, and kept at a distance from police cars it would look like I had just another passenger on the back with a very large, orange helmet. I got on the bike and kick started the Yamaha. Joe then hopped on and for some reason was carrying a long stick.

It was getting late in the afternoon, with the sun about ready to be tucked in for the night. Our adrenaline was flying, while old Yammie whined with two on his back. We were quite amused to see the response on the faces of those we passed. Evidently the pumpkin helmet was not as convincing as we thought it would be for it was not passing the inspection of the pedestrians and cars that we encountered on old Route 282. It was hard not to laugh ourselves at the silly sight that we had become. We thought it was a shame to work our way back to Coatesville on the country roads to avoid the policeman's detection. So we took a big gamble and went into the heart of Downingtown, where our audience would naturally increase. Joe was using his stick to tap on the windows of the cars which we zipped by. We wanted all to notice our late TRICK OR TREAT exploits.

Fortunately, Joe used enough discretion not to gain the attention of the Downingtown police car going in the opposite direction or later the State Trooper who was parked at a gas station. I breathed a sigh of relief when I glanced in the mirror and saw that as we passed the State Trooper he did not follow the Halloween Phantom. However, we took that as a hint to get back on the country roads for certainly we could not press our luck any further on Highway 30.

It was getting dark, the Cyclops headlight was on, and we were racing to get home before we froze. My exposed hands gripped the handlebars, but with no feeling from the frostbite. My face was red and my eyes were iced. Joe likewise was freezing and suffering from the chilling effects of a helmet which when put on was still quite moist from the pumpkin mush.

My mind wandered as we made the last turn into my father's neighborhood. It had been four hours since I started my ride around the block. Would dad kill me? The only consolation I could think of was that my dad would be so hot that my freezing body would benefit from the global warming. As I shifted, I could distinguish the outline of my dad standing on the front porch. What type of greeting would we receive? Would he appreciate my TRICK or would I be in for a real TREAT?

As I pulled in the driveway, my dad screamed to my stepmother, who was already watching our entrance through the kitchen window, "Honey, take a look at these two kooks!" She had noticed that I had someone on the back of the bike and that the helmet looked rather funny even from the distance. My dad and my stepmother could not contain themselves when Joe and I got off the bike and they saw it was old Joe-in-the-lantern. We were so cold and must have looked ridiculous. Dad's wrath was appeased when Joe could not at first get the pumpkin off his head because it was frozen so tightly to his head and hair. We both went inside and began to defrost while Dad and Lynn continued to laugh as Joe gradually worked the makeshift helmet off his head.

This was the one time when Joe's presence and actions were able to save my hide and to propitiate the wrath of my father who had every right to tar and feather me for my monkey-business. Instead of dad's anger being vented, it was appeased. Dad and Lynn warmly accepted us. I knew I would never ride the Yamaha again, but that did not seem to faze me. I was just glad to be inside where there was heat. Dad put a jacket around me and Lynn made us each a cup of hot cocoa. As we thawed out, I thought of how next Halloween I would leave the TRICKS to someone else, and stick with the TREATS.

THIS CHAPTER IS DEDICATED to my Dad and to Grandma Lynn who have put up with my many shenanigans and hooligan friends for many years. I take full responsibility for his gray hair and receding hairline. This chapter is also dedicated to my Texas Elsinore friend, Jack Thompson, who I could never catch for he always had one more gear!

CHAPTER FOUR

FROSHMAN THE SNOWMAN

It was January of my junior year in college. It was great to be back in school after the lengthy Christmas break. It is funny how you cannot wait for Christmas break and then with equal eagerness, cannot wait to get back to the routine of college life! This night, January 26, 1980 reminded me very much of my first visit to Elizabethtown College in 1977, when on Superbowl Sunday I loaded my VW bug with all my belongings and made the one hour and fourteen minute trip to start my first semester of college. That cold, snowy night my mother and stepfather followed me in their Chevy pick-up truck with additional items that I could not fit in my VW. I can still, as clear as night, see my mother's tears as she said good-bye and watched her first-born son enter a new phase of his life. I don't know which was bigger, her tears or the snowflakes which were adding new landscapes to an already pretty campus.

This night it also was snowing, but even more intensely. If it snowed enough I was planning to get my skis out to ski in the dell or out by the baseball field. The last time we had a big snowstorm I skied and did not get back to the dorm until 1:00 in the morning. Wayne "Hound Dog" McCullough, the RA of Brinser 2North was not too pleased with me "forgetting" to take my skis off as I clanked and slid down the halls with skis and poles in full skiing form. I have to admit that my actions that night were somewhat obnoxious.

The snow continued all night at a blizzard's pace. The next morning it was breathtaking to see 4 feet of snow dumped all over the campus. It was perfectly quiet, except for the trucks trying to plow the snow off the roads as well as the shovels banging as efforts were being made to throw salt over the walkways. The students were soon notified that all classes were called off for the day due to the conditions making it too difficult for those living off campus to get to the campus. This was great news because I was already behind in my work, despite the spring semester being just two weeks old. Maybe I could catch up.

After lunch, the cafeteria had permitted the students to borrow the eating trays to go traying on the hills by the quarry. That interested me, but there were a bunch of guys who wanted to play football behind the dorms. I chose the tackle football game, which would be quite safe with 4 feet of padding beneath us. We had a blast trying to run pass patterns and then stuffing one another into the snow. A bunch of girls joined in which made the game even more interesting. We were all exhausted after just a few minutes of competition. I made one diving interception where I was able to hold the ball up over the snow for the catch.

After the football game, Dave, nicknamed Beersie, and I walked down to the Jay's Nest and campus post office. Dave was going to try out for the Blue Jays baseball team and had a decent throwing arm. As we neared the post office we both picked up some snow and formed several snowballs. We then thought it fun and challenging to see how many people we could hit. Of course, I threw out the first ball. What took place was like a chain reaction, our whole game snowballed, and it wasn't too long before it looked like everyone in sight was engaged in the Battle of the Bulge. Dave and I met our Waterloo, however, when a bunch of sourpuss's didn't want to play our little game and ganged up on us. Fortunately, we had stockpiled our snowballs and were able to hold them off with our comet-like throws. They had somewhat iced over and were quite a weapon at short range. We were able to keep most of our adversaries from coming within 75 feet of us. We also enjoyed selectively hitting the innocent powder puffs that were passing through the area. Some seemed to enjoy it, while others thought we were quite immature.

It felt great to get back to the dorms and get out of the wet and snow-ridden clothes and into some dry, warm clothes. I hadn't gotten much schoolwork done, nothing new, but it sure was a great day. At that moment the hall phone rang and it was for me. When I got to the phone I answered it and heard a handful of girls singing. They had made up a song to invite Dave and me to come to the Dell outside of their dorm that night for another snowball fight, which would then be followed with some hot cocoa and goodies. I immediately accepted the invitation and told them we would be down right at 7:00 p.m. After hanging up the phone, I laughed at the funny snowman song that they had made up, and then thought, how immature.

Dave and I had dinner together that night. In the cafeteria I told Dave of our snowy invitation. Dave said it sounded great, but asked what we would do about our gym duty that night from 7:00 p.m. to 10:00 p.m. I had totally forgotten about our work schedule in the equipment room for that evening. I said, "Oh no! What are we going to do?" I didn't even know the names of those who had invited us, for the girls did not want to relinquish that information over the phone. I couldn't even tell them that we couldn't be there. It was then, as if the light bulb went on; that I had an idea concerning how I could keep both of my obligations. Their snowman song was the catalyst! A snowman we would give them!

"Dave, let's go up to my room and pick up all of my wet clothes that I was wearing today and let's go down to the Dell and make a snow man that would give the appearance of me in the dark shadows of the Dell." Dave thought it was worth a shot and that it might serve as a temporary substitute and conversation piece. We both had determined we would shut the gym down early and see if we could stir up another snowball fight between the two girl's dorms late that evening.

Once in the Dell with my snowman's wardrobe we quickly began to create Froshman the Snowman. It didn't take too long to stuff enough snow down the trousers to give form to the lower torso. However, it was quite challenging to find just the right length sticks to fit into the arms of my red jacket to give some life to our amputee. Finally, we placed a glove into each sleeve and on top of Froshman's icy head a ski cap to give a convincing look to our masterpiece. Dave and I grinned at each other. All we needed was a lightning bolt to send life into our snowy creation. We were greatly impressed with ourselves as we rushed to the other side of campus to work in the gym. Once we got to the gym, we saw a note on the outside door that Mr. Erb had closed the gym for the night due to the blizzard like conditions from the night before. Fantastic, back to the Dell!

As Dave and I walked down the snow-banked road towards the Dell we heard the screams of a handful of girls. The closer we came to the Royer Dormitory, which was adjacent to the Dell, the more we could distinguish their message. The kicker was, they were addressing me, and calling for me to come to the lounge of Royer. It didn't take Dave and me long to realize that the girls thought our Snowman was actually me and that they were talking to our inanimate friend. This was too good to be true. Not wanting to be seen, we both ducked behind the 6-foot snowdrifts that were piled up from the wings of the snowplows. We then tried to locate the room from where the voices were coming. It appeared that they were coming from somewhere in the middle section of the second floor. The lights were off in their rooms, but their windows were open. The girls were just tantalizing the poor fellow in the Dell.

Since they were hollering for me to come in, we deemed it best to honor their invitation and attempted to climb on to the ledge beneath their window above the front porch of the dorm and give them a shocking face-to-face greeting. With the snow piled up near the dorm's entrance we figured we could climb up the wrought iron porch and maneuver ourselves to one of their windows. It sounded like a solid plan, but Dave slipped as he climbed and ripped his jeans. I felt a little jittery climbing up onto the roof of the porch, but neither of us wanted to go through the lounge where the RA would give us a hard time and possibly not allow us to visit the girls that we still had not met officially. I could not pull myself completely up on to the slippery roof and jumped backward into the snow pile. I told Dave to climb in and then to come to the side entrance of the building and let me in, so we both could finish our mission in spooking the girls who obviously were still trying to conceal their identity from us. Dave slipped again and seeing some girls returning to the dorm jumped down as well.

The side doors were usually locked at this time of night, but we decided it was worth a shot. The girls were continuing their high-shrilled conversation with Froshman the Snowman, but we knew our time was running short to strike with optimum effect. At the side of the building we pulled on the door; we were in luck; the doors were unlocked. We quickly ran up the steps streaked with water from the dripping boots of an army of girls and found our way down the hall to where we thought we could match the voices of the girls. It didn't take any Sherlock Holmes to find the loud room. We knocked on the door. They said, "Come in," not knowing who stood behind their metal shield. Were they ever surprised! Their mouths dropped! Their faces were Rudolph red when they saw us. Were they ever embarrassed by their childish game of hide and seek.

After we broke the ice with them, they mentioned that they had thought that the man in the Dell was me. I explained that it wasn't me for we had to work in the gym. I told them we were sorry that we were a few minutes late for the festivities and that we had come straight to their dormitory from the gym. They then asked who was in the Dell. My countenance changed to a very serious, concerned look after their question. I said, "How long has he been out there?" They replied, "For at least twenty minutes." I told them that with the wind chill factor, the temperature outside must be nearing below zero degrees and that it would not be good for anyone to stand in one place for any amount of time without the fear of getting frostbite. They seemed to understand the danger. Being the good Samaritan that I was, I nobly told the girls that we would go out, see who it was, and inquire as to what he was doing standing out in the cold. They thought it was a manly thing for us to do and were quite touched for our concern and compassion for this unknown individual.

Dave and I quickly walked outside the dorm doing everything in our power not to bust into tears laughing, but we knew that if we could just keep our composure that the best was yet to come. The girls watched out their windows, this time with their lights on. Dave and I went into the gloomy, dark Dell and entered into a conversation with our chilly friend. After several minutes, Dave and I returned to the Dorm and met with the girls.

With very dejected frowns on our faces we mentioned to the girls that the fellow in the Dell was a freshman by the name of John and that he and his girlfriend had a meltdown. We then continued to inform the girls that he was so heartbroken that he saw no reason for living and that he was just going to stand out there all night until he froze to death. I then concluded by saying, "Girls, you would not believe how cold he is; he is as cold as ice." They had no idea how accurate that statement was!

The girls looked like they would do anything to help John overcome the cold heartedness of his girlfriend and her untimely Dear John letter. I said to the girls, "Maybe if we all worked together we could persuade John to come in out of the cold. Why don't we ask all the girls on the hall to open their windows and on the count of three, in unison, scream, please John come in?" They thought it was a splendid idea. Dave almost lost control of his stoicism and walked away from the conversation. Hopefully none of the girls saw him fighting off his hysterics. The girls quickly covered the hall to inform the other girls of what was happening and how they could help by going to their window and screaming out to John to come in from the cold. The hall was buzzing! After a few minutes most all of the girls on the hall were stationed at their windows, I screamed, "One, Two, Three" and then in perfect unison a wave of voices resounded over the snow, "Please John come in!" I said loudly, "Again girls" and again they screamed, but this time even louder. It would not be until the next day that I would find out that their voices carried and were heard by others in nearby dorms.

After the second loud roar, one of the girls screeched, "He moved!" That almost finished me off, I was about to come unglued! I quickly met in the hall and gathered the girls together. I tried to encourage them that he had at least moved, as the one girl noticed and that there was hope. Now we would have to try it one more time, but this time they would have to coordinate their efforts with Dave and I, while we would be outside trying to apply our persuasive powers one more time with John. Perhaps this one-two punch would work.

Well at this time, one of the girls began to wise up to our monkey-business and began questioning the validity of John and the sad story. She had not seen him move and was not so convinced that John would ever move, except on a hot, sunny day. I quickly intercepted her and went into her room and asked if she would play along with our prank. She agreed after some hesitation and gained more confidence as we asked her to join us on our next counseling session with John. With the girls screaming out the window and Dave and I and our female accomplice talking with John, we were still not able to make a breakthrough. We returned to the dorm with the bad news that John was not going to budge despite everyone's efforts. I also reinforced to them that John seemed to be critically cold. I then convinced them that immediate action must be taken. One of the girls, a rather heavy set black girl on the hall, quickly volunteered to call the campus security to come to the rescue. I agreed that that was what was needed. She then ran to the phone and in a very excited voice told the campus police that there was a man in the Dell that was nearly frozen to death and that they needed to come immediately. They responded that they would be right there.

I thought perhaps now that the problem was under control that Dave and I should get on our way. Then the thought hit me, that it was my very expensive jacket on old Froshman the Snowman. My mom would shoot me if I lost that coat. I would have to stay and somehow seek to recover my clothes.

Within minutes the campus police car was in front of the dorm in all its glory, rivaling even the Christmas lights in the girls lounge. Out jumped what looked like Barney Fife's brother. He was beaming with self-importance. By this time there was quite a commotion at Royer Dorm. The entire dorm was now looking on at the scene with great curiosity. I met the policeman and explained that I just happened to be walking by when he drove up in his cruiser entering from the wrong direction on the one-way street to save precious seconds. I described to him that some of the girls were concerned about some student in the Dell who they thought might be a prospect for a cryonic project. The officer and I then turned and looked toward the Dell. Surprised and alarmed, I said, "Oh, there he is Officer."

I wanted to give every impression that this was my first journey of the night into the Dell and that I was just as much uninformed regarding the dilemma as he was. He turned on his large flashlight and headed down into the Dell. I followed by his side asking him if there was anything I could do to help. When we got within the range of the flash light of Froshman the Snowman, the face of the policeman turned as white as old John's. He was furious to see that it was only a snowman and that he had been made to look like a fool. To complicate things it appeared that he may have called for a backup and/or an ambulance. I said, "Sir, this is terrible! Someone should have looked into this more carefully before they called you." He agreed sternly. I quickly added, "Officer, whoever did this should pay some consequences for snowing the police." He agreed again. I then asked, "How about, if you don't mind, I take the clothes off the snowman and dispose of them? For this would serve as some form of fitting retribution to whoever used their nice clothes in this prank." He smiled, and said, "Good idea, why don't you just keep them." I said, "Thanks, in fact they look like my size."

As we dismantled Froshman the Snowman, the girls in Royer dorm went into hysterics. I walked back to the police car carrying my clothes. The officer on duty wanted to get out of there as quickly as possible, but had to report immediately to the dispatch that it was only a snowman and that he would not need a backup or an ambulance. I waved good-bye.

The girls now clearly recognized that they had been snowed as well. They seemed to be caught between anger and laughter. Dave and I deemed it wise to head back to our dormitory quickly before we were snowed and feathered by a dorm of giggling but potentially hostile girls. We told the girls we had to get back to study and then left waving good-bye to the remains of **FROSHMAN THE SNOWMAN**.

THIS CHAPTER IS DEDICATED to all my classmates at Elizabethtown College and especially my roommates Scott Kennedy, Jeff Miller, Don Warner, Rick Quinn, Jim Schlosser and Al Heney. Sorry guys about the messy room, and to Rick for throwing his tennis racket. Dr. Dave this chapter is also dedicated to you! What a blessing to follow your travels in the *Etownian*.

CHAPTER FIVE

JONAH AND THE ENGAGEMENT RING

F inally, December 19, 1981, the day had arrived that school would let out for Christmas Break. Being some 700 miles away from Allissa had been quite a challenge during this my first semester in grad school. The only winner in the situation was Southern Bell. We had been calling each other almost daily, while counting the days down to my last day of school before the long drive home. We were both excited knowing that over this Christmas holiday season I was going to engage Allissa officially to be my wife, with the wedding to take place some time in June of 1982. Along with trying to make some arrangements to get home, I had been diligently praying, seeking the Lord to give me some special way of presenting the diamond ring to Allissa that would be most memorable. I had several crazy ideas about how to give it to her, yet had no peace on any of them. One thing I was certain about, and that was the timing for my presentation which would either be Christmas Eve or Christmas morning.

There was a student I had met who needed a ride home to the same area where Allissa lived. We were trying to mastermind some plan to resurrect my 66 Dodge pickup truck out of the parking lot of Bob Jones University in Greenville, South Carolina. It needed some work done to the front-end alignment, which was eating up front tires at a very quick rate. The truck also needed to be inspected in PA as well as an insurance payment made before I could really drive it. Thus, Dennis Wolf and I both decided to keep our ears open to hear if anyone was going our way and could give us a ride. We would be more than glad to share the traveling expense.

Dennis, the day before we were to head home, had met some girl whose dad was coming down from New York State who said he would be willing to bring home a couple of her friends if they needed a ride. She said her dad would have to charge us each $50 for the ride. I thought at first that this was somewhat high because I could drive my truck home if it was running properly for about $60. I thought if I asked Dennis to chip in $50.00, I could have the truck repaired and we could drive it home. After some deliberation and not knowing anyone in SC who could fix my truck I reluctantly said, "Dennis, I believe that the ride from the man from NY looks like the best arrangement." He agreed, and I took $50.00 of my last $62.59 and returned to tell the girl from NY to count us in for the ride home.

We would be leaving early the next morning for the fifteen-hour drive home. I could hardly wait to pull off! I had called Allissa the previous night and told her that I would be seeing her late the next night. I then informed her that we wouldn't have to be apart ever again for I was not planning to return for the spring semester because I was $1000 behind on my school bill. I was in some ways very glad to be $1000 behind, so that I could move up to Allissa's neck of the woods, find a job, get married, and then return to Greenville in the Fall of 1982 and continue my studies for the ministry. The only problem with my plans was that I just wasn't having any peace about staying out next semester, especially after Dr. Bob's Christmas farewell sermon. He preached on how Jonah ran from God's will and paid the fare because of his disobedience. Dr. Jones warned that, "Some of you students are making plans not to return next semester. You are not trusting God to provide and are running from the will of God." For some reason I felt like Jonah. I wasn't running from my studies but from the heartache caused by being so far away from Allissa. I could hardly stand the idea of being separated from her for another five months. Fortunately, there was no way I could get the $1000 and stay in school.

The next morning we met in front of one of the girl's dorms where we met Mr. Horn-blower who had driven his truck down from New York the day before. He had an older truck with a semi-homemade looking camper over the back of the truck bed. It looked like it would be waterproof if it didn't rain, but with no heat in the back, could lend itself for a long, cold ride home.

Mr. Horn-blower was somewhat miffed over the amount of luggage his daughter wanted to bring home and to complicate matters she had committed her dad to take seven other students home with multiple drop-offs on the way. When you added her father, mother and younger brother to the list, there would be eleven heading home in the truck which meant three up front and eight sardines in the back, plus everyone's luggage. Sharon's girlfriends were loaded for bear, you would have thought they were moving back home for life with all their luggage!

Mr. Horn-blower looked very hesitantly at the entire situation. All I could think of was seven times $50.00, or $350.00. This fellow was going to rack it in from driving all of the livestock. Not a bad deal for him, especially since he had to make the drive for his daughter anyway. I kept my mouth shut and began to kick myself for not getting my truck ready for the long trek home.

What seemed like hours to load up the truck was actually only forty-five minutes. We finally all hopped in the back of the truck and I watched Mr. Horn-blower shut the door to the cage. I was not looking forward to the fifteen-hour drive, cramped in the bed of the truck with a bunch of people I did not know, but at this point had no other choice. We all introduced ourselves and began to small talk about our majors, classes, professors, etc. Dennis was girl crazy so he did not mind being the only eligible man in the truck with seven single girls. I made it immediately clear that I was a marked man and that I was planning to be engaged in just seven short days. I thought that was important to do because I sensed that Miss Heffer, the home economics major and minor, liked me.

Once on the road, I could tell the truck was having some strain placed upon it with all the weight in the back which I guessed with the heavy home-made camper top, luggage and people was weighing in at a minimum of 3,000 pounds.

We were on the road for only two hours when we began to smell something burning. We began knocking and then pounding on the window between the cab and us. Mr. Horn-blower immediately looked in his right rear view mirror and saw a cloud of smoke coming from the rear of the truck. He immediately pulled over on the shoulder of I-85.

I noticed the smoke and immediately banged the door open and began helping the girls out of the back. I thought the whole truck was about to explode, especially with the fire so near the gas tank. In light of the risk, I also knew I had to get everyone out as quickly as possible. To my surprise, the first person to fly out of the truck and run for cover was Dennis. With him out of the way, I helped each of the girls out of the truck, they then ran for cover, and then I sprinted away from the truck.

By that time, a car had pulled over and a man jumped out with a small fire extinguisher and quickly put out the fire near the rear axle area. Were we ever relieved to escape what could have been a real death-trap! Poor Dennis, any hopes of

41

advancement with the girls was shattered when he sought first to save his own skin and to run from the scene. I didn't consider myself to be any hero, but the girls were all enamored with what they thought was quite a chivalrous deed. Before I could brace myself, Miss Heffer gave me a big hug for saving her life.

A church van pulled up onto the shoulder while Mr. Horn-blower was trying to figure out what had happened. It wasn't a flat tire, but appeared to have something to do with the weight of the truck damaging the brakes or axle or something. I'm not very mechanical so I stayed away from the inspection and analysis. All I knew was that it was going to take us a little longer getting home.

The man in the church van talked with us and said it was awfully dangerous for us to stand on the side of the highway. He stated that he would be glad to give us a ride to their Christian school while the truck was being fixed and could make a call to a friend to tow the truck to his friend's shop.

What a blessing and how kind of him to stop for us. Mr. Horn-blower agreed and said he would stay back with the truck and wait for the tow truck and that after the truck was fixed would come to the Christian school and pick us up. We all hopped in the van and got off into the suburban section of Charlotte, NC. Psychologically it was nice to be out of South Carolina, but I knew all too well that we had only traveled two hours and still had thirteen hours to go. Every hour of delay here would cause our arrival to be pushed back into the wee hours of the night, technically morning.

After weaving through traffic we finally arrived at a rather large Christian school with several hundred students in attendance. The man explained our situation to the principal. The principal was very kind and since it was nearing lunchtime invited all of us to eat lunch in the school's cafeteria. That was the first good news I had heard all day. I was starving! Their invitation would also supplement my very limited meal budget for the trip home.

After lunch, we heard the bad news. Mr. Horn-blower dejectedly said that the fire had done some serious damage to the truck and it needed a part that no one in the area had, so they had to order it and that the soonest it could get there would be early the next morning. I couldn't believe it! I didn't know if I was the Jonah causing the waves or if the Lord wanted to impress the messages of Job which I had been reading for my devotions that morning into my actual life experience. What a choice, Jonah or Job for a day! We were all very disappointed to have our trip delayed a full day.

Both the pastor and principal of the church and school recognized our dilemma and graciously volunteered to find housing for each of us for that night. They truly made us feel at home. I called Allissa and told her the bad news. She was really set back by the change in the arrival time, but there was nothing I could do to change it.

The principal, who was a graduate of Piedmont Bible College, and somewhat familiar with Bob Jones University, asked if I would speak to the students and give my testimony of how I became a Christian as well as to preach a message. I quickly said yes, and asked how soon I would need to be ready to speak. He said when the bell rings; which would be at the end of the lunch and recess hour, which would be in about twenty minutes.

I frantically tried to put some ideas together for my message, and tried to think of any projects I had worked on in my first semester of grad school. The most edifying thing I could think of was a recent study in Systematic Theology which dealt with all the lists of sins in the New Testament. Certainly that would bless their hearts. I also had fresh in my mind some pointed illustrations and stories that certain preachers had used in chapel at Bob Jones University. All I needed to do was to adapt some illustrations to my sin list project and we would be homiletically set.

The twenty minutes flew by and it didn't take but a few minutes for the principal to work through the preliminaries of chapel to introduce a young preacher by the name of Will Sin. Everyone laughed at his clever introduction. Fortunately, that was not the first time that the Will Sin introduction was used and I am sure not the last.

I was very familiar with giving my testimony, and not so familiar with preaching, so what I did in midstream was just give my testimony, highlighting at different points the sin lists and using several illustrations from the well-known evangelists at BJU. It was quite a mumbo-jumbo sermon! There was no outline, no theme, no introduction, no real solid Biblical content, but the Lord still used it as I had prayed for Him to bless despite my inability. A fleeting thought passed that my message was a poor reflection on my future alma mater and the quality training they provided.

At the end of my sermon the Lord led me to use an illustration about a young Christian lady who was dating an unbeliever and ultimately married him against everyone's counsel, and consequently became a statistic when he later left her. With that illustration in place I was ready for my two-fold invitation: salvation for the unbelieving listener and the importance for the high school students to date Christians that are living for God, and to avoid being unequally yoked. Being a Christian school, I didn't know how many, if any, of the kids were lost and had never entered into a vital relationship with Christ.

When I asked with their heads bowed and eyes closed how many were not saved and would like to trust the Lord as their personal Savior, five hands went quickly in the air. I asked those who raised their hands to come up front and stay after chapel was dismissed so the principal and I could talk with them. All five would trust Christ that day. It thrilled my heart to see the Lord work.

I then asked the group if God was dealing with them about their dating life. I asked if any were dating an unsaved person. If so, I asked if they would raise their hands for prayer. Several of the students raised their hands and to my surprise, one of the teachers in the school raised her hand and was fighting back tears. Later, I found out that she was substituting for one of the ladies who had just had a baby, and that she was going through a real struggle about dating an unsaved man. That day she decided to turn her dating over to the Lord and to terminate her relationship with her boyfriend based on the authority of II Corinthians 6:14. It was an exciting opportunity! I then could see more clearly why the Lord allowed our truck to breakdown, but I still resented the delay in Ninevah.

Following chapel I was introduced to one of the students whose parents had volunteered to have me spend the night at their place. He was a very troubled young fellow. So, I took it as an opportunity to be an encouragement to him. He had a gym class so I went with him and played basketball with him and his classmates. It was one of those days where I couldn't miss. They thought I was Larry Bird.

I was humored and at the same time fought back some pride in my victories on the court over these Junior High munchkins. After playing I talked about the Lord with a few of the kids that had athletic abilities, but who did not appear to have a Christian testimony. After witnessing to them, two trusted the Lord as their Savior.

After school, David's mother came to pick him up as well as their surprise guest. They lived in a nice little development in the suburbs of Charlotte. I met David's father and we had a nice time getting to know each other as we enjoyed a great home cooked meal!

Following that we went back to the Christian school to watch the varsity basketball game. At the game, a handful of the students came over and talked with me. It was quite evident that our misfortunes had by now been told to all the parents and we were the news of the school. One of the boys who was saved that afternoon played on the basketball team. He was just beaming. I told him to have a good game and to play for the Lord. They got beat badly, but it was with great joy I could walk out of that gym knowing that some eternal victories had been won that day.

Back at David's house, I got ready for bed. I was exhausted. David's dad, however, wanted to talk a little bit more and seemed to be very burdened about his own spiritual life. He was a Vietnam Vet and was struggling with false guilt over his activities in Vietnam. I was able to encourage him that it is not sinful to defend your country or the rights of another country and that unfortunately at times war is needed and people are killed.

I tried to explain the commandment, "*Thou shalt not kill*" to the best of my knowledge, making the differentiation between kill and murder. He had evidently killed many in Vietnam. His wife interrupted us and said it was getting late. She went over the last details of light switches, breakfast menus, towels, etc and was the perfect hostess. Then she dropped a bomb on me. "By the way, my husband often has nightmares of the war and wakes up in a cold sweat screaming, in fact, he has even picked up his 38 caliber pistol and he hides behind the bed pointing it at anything he thinks is the enemy. So don't worry if you hear anything unusual. Good night!"

Now how could I sleep on that! Good Night! What if he has a bad dream and sees me, an unfamiliar person in his house, and tries to shoot me! I decided that regardless of any physical discomfort, that I would not get up in the night to use the bathroom down the hallway; and that I would do everything in my power not to make a noise or even turn over until I heard the alarm go off in the morning and heard them talking. Needless to say, I slept very little that night. If that wasn't enough they had some obnoxious wooden bird that made his presence known on the hour. Coo-Coo! Coo-Coo!

"Good Morning! Did you sleep well?" I lied, "Great night, thanks." I went to school in the carpool with David and was reunited with my fellow travelers.

It was 10:00 a.m. by the time the truck was fixed and ready to get back on the road, which considering all the factors was a real miracle. We said goodbye to all our new friends and excitedly got back in the truck and on the road again. It was a crisp, clear December day!

I pulled out my Bible and began to read Job again for my devotions. For one of my classes we had to read the entire Bible through during the course of the year, so I was killing two birds with one stone.

Just as I was getting settled down and about an hour into our trip, we heard this loud bang and felt the truck swerving on the road. It didn't take any Einstein to figure out he had blown a rear tire. Fortunately, he was able to pull safely the thumping truck off I-77. The cars and trucks whisked by and shook the truck. Mr. Horn-blower was not too pleased to see his tire flat. Dennis didn't help any by his comment that it was only flat on one side and that all he needed to do was to turn it upside down. Dennis was beginning to get on everyone's nerves with his dry sense of humor that was apparently on a non-stop flight to PA.

Mr. Horn-blower had a spare and put it on, but it was under the luggage. I could not help but think what would prevent another tire from exploding with all the weight on the back of the truck. He assured me, however, that these were heavy-duty tires. Back on the road and back into Job. I had been praying silently for the Lord to protect us because Mr. Horn-blower was trying to make up time by really pushing it down the hills. We all had our own projected times and places to meet with family and friends on the route home. We were on the road no more than forty-five minutes when we heard another large bang!!! I couldn't believe it, but then again I could. He was able to pull the truck over, but we all knew that there was not another spare and we were several miles from an old country road exit.

I again asked the Lord, "Am I the Jonah on this trip?" I began to think aloud with Dennis that maybe the two of us should seek another way home, but neither of us could think of a reasonable alternative as well as a tactful way to tell Mr. Horn-blower that he was half crazy to attempt a drive with the load he had.

Mr. Horn-blower was able to wave someone down who kindly took him and the first flat tire to a tire place up in the mountains. Mr. Horn-blower returned with a tire, which he made clear to all that he found at a price as high as those mountains. He quickly replaced the flat with the new tire and said he would pull over as soon as we got to a larger city where he could match the new tire at a lower price and put it on the other side so that we would be riding on two brand new tires. It made good sense to us, but we were all looking at our watches, especially when several tire companies did not have that mountain variety tire in stock, I think it was called a Flintstone Radial. Finally he found a place that stocked that brand, and at a slightly reduced price had that tire mounted.

In my heart, I was starting to feel bad for Mr. Horn-blower and the amount of money he had already spent on the truck. I thought justice had been more than served for what I had wrongly and prematurely judged as greed on his part to collect $50 from each of us at the onset of the trip. I also wondered if they just throw me overboard, if they would then have a smooth trip home.

We had lunch and then with the two new tires were rolling with a new confidence that the truck would make it home. Late in the evening, we stopped at McDonalds for dinner. Several of the girls chipped in to purchase some burgers and fries for me when they realized I wasn't going to eat with the group and figured out I had no more money.

We were on schedule to arrive in Harrisburg, PA at approximately 10:00 p.m. Two of the girls, who were sisters, were going to meet their parents at one of the exits in Harrisburg. I was fading, but once in Harrisburg I knew we were no more than four hours away from Allissa's. There was a sense of relief in all of our hearts to be finally in our home state and in familiar territory. We arrived at the appointed exit right at 10:00 p.m. but there were no parents to pick up the two sisters. We waited and waited until the girls realized that we were at the wrong exit. They had told their parents to meet them at Exit 15, but what they had really meant to tell them was to meet them at the Route 15 exit. These were two entirely different stops. In the future, someone will need to invent cell phones.

We were all tired and very anxious to move on. It was also getting very cold, with the temperature dropping to ten degrees, and the foot of snow on the ground added an additional reminder that it was cold out there! Finally, Mr. Horn-blower moved ahead to Route 15 which was some 10 miles away. Again, I said, "Lord, why? Am I the problem? Am I the Jonah? Why can't we find these people?" Once at Route 15, we waited and waited and then drove through the figure eight's to see if they were waiting on any of the nearby connectors to Route 15. Finally, the girls decided to call home. Fortunately, their brother was home and he relayed the message that their parents had just called as well, and that they were parked off Exit 15. Once Mr. Horn-blower got word where they were, he backtracked quickly to Exit 15, hoping that they would not criss-cross us again which was actually what had happened before when we went to see if they were at the other exit. This time they had stayed put, and to the cheers of all, the weeping sisters identified their car when we neared the exit ramp. They jumped out of the truck and embraced their parents and got their luggage. We all said good bye and wished them a Merry Christmas.

I called Allissa quickly to tell her that we had a two hour delay in Harrisburg and that we should roll into Columbia Cross Roads at approximately 4:00 a.m. I asked her just to leave the door unlocked and I would just go to my room and would see her in the morning. She was crushed; she had been watching every car come down her country road with the hope that it was her prince in shining armor. She had no idea that her prince, when he arrived would not have slept much for forty-eight hours and that he looked like an emaciated scarecrow with rings around his eyes that would make even Saturn jealous. At 4:15 a.m., after convincing Mr. Horn-blower to go the extra 6 miles to drop me off at Allissa's house, for he had originally wanted Allissa to come and pick me up at Highway 6, I arrived at my destination. Needless to say I was relieved, but drained. I walked to the house and glanced at the thermometer on the porch, it was below zero.

I took my suitcase and luggage to the guestroom, which was her Brother Steve's old room. All I wanted to do was hide the engagement ring, because I knew Allissa would snoop around to see if I had brought it. You cannot keep any secrets around the Isbell girls.

I had previously brought the ring up over Thanksgiving when I had taken some cuts from school with Al Heney and Rick Shadel. She had expected and hoped then that I would make our marriage plans official with the presentation of the engagement ring. I was too thickheaded at the time to pick up on her signals, and in fact, I was going to present it to her then, but I wanted to do it in such a manner that would have a lasting and memorable impact. Nothing had come to mind then to do it just right. I thought when the ring is small that the presentation has to be really big. Since then I had been praying for a creative, memorable way to give her the ring at Christmas, but still had no good ideas. I quickly took the ring box out of my bag and looked for a place to put it in the room. Aha, I said to myself, Steve's gun cabinet. She would never look in the drawer of the cabinet. Mission accomplished, now I could sleep in peace.

Several hours later I could hear the family down stairs talking and laughing, and could hear the voice of Jarvis, Allissa's brother-in-law, joking and teasing with Allissa's mom. I could have slept forever, but was riding on adrenaline to see Allissa and the family. They had all warmly received me not only into their home, but also into their hearts. I loved my future family and in-laws. They had all been alerted by Allissa that I would probably pop the question and break out the ring at Christmas. The likelihood of this brought additional teasing and razzing from her brothers and sisters.

We all had a super time, except for the time at Ted's Christmas program. The school choir was excellently prepared to sing a few traditional carols, but for the most part would sing some contemporary rock songs that at best were irreverent from my perspective, but from theirs and especially in a public school were probably extremely conservative and tempered. Despite their stellar performance from an earthly perspective, I was the only one who was left in their seat at the standing ovation. Poor Ted, he didn't understand why his future brother in law frowned at some of his music and his Christian Rock Band. Well at least the family knew then if they didn't know before, that they were going to have a real oddball for their son-in-law. Likeable perhaps, but odd and very narrow!

Allissa's father had a special dog which had disappeared. So Allissa and I kept our ears open to hear if anyone had any pups for sale. Sure enough one of Allissa's friends had a black mutzski who had just had pups. We fell in love with one little fellow and picked it up to give to Allissa's dad for an early Christmas surprise. He was surprised all right, perhaps too surprised.

Finally the time had come for me to ask Allissa's father if I could marry his daughter. We were both enjoying one of the college bowl games being played before Christmas. It was a perfect setting as we both sat on the couch talking about the game. During each commercial I built up more nerve to ask him the big question. Finally, after a touchdown, and realizing that there would be a good three minutes of commercials, I said "Mr. Isbell, I would like to have your permission to marry your daughter Allissa." He was real quiet, and being a man of few words, said, "Yes, if you will take good care of her and provide for her." The game resumed and not wanting to miss the kickoff I said, "I will take good care of her." He said, "Good." We continued to watch our game and have a super time together. I think Allissa was eavesdropping in the other room. I think she was thinking that this was going to be a real romantic Hallmark moment, finally during another commercial I went out to the kitchen to get some ice cream and told Allissa that her dad had said yes, that I could marry her. She was real excited. I was too, but had to get back to the game, priorities.

The next day was Christmas Eve. Steve, Allissa's brother, came down from New York that morning to get a load of wood as well as to pick up his gun cabinet that he finally wanted to transport back to the Air Force base some three hours away from Allissa's place. Steve and I had a good time together. He had been sizing me up at each of our visits to see if I was the one for his sister. I think I passed his test, but so had seventeen of Allissa's last thirty-five serious boyfriends. Before he was to leave, he asked if I could help him carry the gun cabinet down from his old room and place it on the back of the truck with all the firewood. It wasn't heavy, just awkward. We got it loaded and tied down on the pickup truck. He needed to get right back for the weatherman was calling for more snow and possible heavy ice storms. It was great to see him, even if it was for just a few minutes.

That night Allissa's parents had been invited to a Christmas Eve party and Ted, Allissa's youngest brother had a meeting with his music band. Allissa was glowing with the high beam of expectancy for our evening alone. It was all lining up as if this would be the special time to present the ring to Allissa, but how to do it with the ultimate mush and romance was still the question. Allissa's mother waved goodbye as they walked out the door to leave us alone. She didn't know I saw her, but I caught her winking to Allissa when she said, "Good Night!" Even her mom was expecting me to give her the ring that night. The pressure was on. What could I do to make it memorable, special, unique, etc.? I excused myself to go up to my guestroom and to think of a game plan on how I could present it to Allissa.

It wasn't like the ring was any Rock of Gibraltar or anything; in fact I hadn't let the poor girl pick it out or hardly look at it to see if she even liked it. How would I know that those things are important to girls? I grew up with only two brothers. I was just excited to have a ring to give her, for that was a real miracle in itself. My mother had given me her engagement ring to present to a former girlfriend, but that relationship did not work out. It was a beautiful ring, and somewhat valuable, but its history and attached memories made the ring somewhat undesirable. After several requests and much prayer, Beanie Klahr, a man in my home church, who owned a jewelry store, offered to give me $500 for the ring as well as the choice of another diamond ring of lesser value. I jumped at his offer, and probably too quickly when it came to the choice of the diamond ring for Allissa.

This all took place in July, and it was with the $500 from the sale of my mother's engagement ring that I was able to pay my first tuition payment to Bob Jones University. Otherwise I could not have entered school at that time. At that time, I thought if I could just make the first payment and get into to the first semester, that some how and some way the Lord would provide the rest. Not only did Beanie give me $500 and another ring, but said that he wanted to mail me a check for $50.00 each month while I was in school. What a blessing, for that was exactly what I needed to make the last nine monthly payments for old Jezebel, my 66 Dodge Pick-up.

Nearing the door of the guestroom I thought all I had to do was get the ring, return downstairs, and simply kneel at Allissa's feet in the kitchen and ask for her hand while gently slipping on the engagement ring followed up with a good smooch. This would have to suffice. It was traditional, conventional, practical, homey and very expedient.

When I entered into my guestroom, Steve's old room, it hit me like a lead balloon that where I had placed the ring was traveling at 95 MPH to New York. As I glared at the empty space created by the missing gun cabinet, I could not believe that I could be that stupid to forget to take the ring out of the cabinet before helping Steve move it. The sad thing was that I hadn't even thought of the ring while we moved it even as I held the drawers together to prevent them from falling out.

Now what? Allissa will be shattered and what about the ring? Could it survive the trip to New York being bounced around and perhaps even out? I ran down stairs to tell Allissa the grave news. After I told her that I was going to give her the ring and that it was gone, she just laughed. Just another one of Will's practical jokes she thought. She determined in her heart that I wasn't going to buffalo her this time. It took several minutes for me to convince her that this was no joke. She came upstairs to look in my room. Big tears were swelling up in her beautiful eyes.

There was only one thing I could do, wait for Steve to get home and then see if the ring made it safely and then to drive up in the snow and ice storm and get the ring. It would be a six-hour round trip, which would give me an arrival time that would correspond with Santa Claus' delivery schedule to the South Pole. Allissa wasn't too hyped up about the idea. We waited and finally Steve returned my call when he got home after receiving the message from his wife. He said, "Will, I can't find the ring in the drawer and I have looked everywhere. I'm sorry! If I find it in the back of the truck I'll let you know, but it appears to be lost. Goodbye and Merry Christmas." We were all but merry!

When Allissa heard the news from Steve she quietly walked into her mother's bedroom and threw herself over the bed and began to cry. I felt terrible as I watched Miss Ahab give new meaning to the waterbed! Here was the girl that proposed to me the first night we met at a Christian camp in Sunbury in June, watching her dream turn into a nightmare. It was there at camp on the porch deck that she had asked me what my plans were when I grew up. I had replied that I was going to be a preacher. I then asked her what her plans were when she grew up, and she quickly replied, a preacher's wife. Here her romantic dreams were dashed. Both of us from that summer night forward knew we had met God's perfect choice for one another's life, but could we overcome this setback?

Then to complicate things I heard the door open and saw the black, wee-wee mutzski pup running wild in the house and up the stairs to where I stood. Mom and dad were home and they had let the pup in. I quickly told them what had happened. Allissa's mother felt very much like Allissa, and Allissa's dad felt very much like I did. Then entered Ted! Ted has the uncanny ability to look on the lighter side of things and sought to humor us. It didn't take Ted long to realize that at this moment we did not need a standup comedian, but a ring, and not one from any bubble gum machine would do as he suggested.

We all waltzed into Steve's room to assess the loss. Allissa's mother, old faithful, said, "Maybe, Will, you put it somewhere else." I quickly said, "No, it was in the cabinet," but to appease her I began to look through my book bag as well as my suitcase. Then to my absolute astonishment, as I went through my clothes I felt a box, and sure enough it was the ring box. I couldn't believe it for I could not remember putting it there. I must have subconsciously that first night, in my exhausted state, gotten out of bed and taken it out of the gun cabinet thinking that maybe she would look there anyway. To be extra safe I wrapped it up in my clothing in my suitcase. Standing there was my future brother-in-law, mother-in-law, father-in-law and the wee-wee-all-over-the-house mutzski and a teary eyed fiancée-to-be. It was a classic Norman Rockwell look. I said, "Allissa give me your hand." I grabbed her hand and in front of them all said, "Put it on. It's yours now, just don't lose it!"

And there you have it, a memorable engagement moment. Romantic? No. Memorable? Yes. The Lord had answered my prayer, but I sure was kicking myself that I had not added in my petition "romantic."

To finish the story about Jonah and the engagement ring. I was to interview for a teaching position in a public school on Friday. It looked quite promising to get in to the school system, but as "fate" would have it we encountered one of the worst ice storms of the winter. We did not dare take the risk to drive. So I missed the interview. The schools were closed anyway and I had to catch my ride to Elizabethtown on Saturday night and be back at Bob Jones University on Monday for the start of finals week which at that time were held after Christmas Break. If they had not been held then, Jonah would have packed his bags before he left and would still be in Pennsylvania seeking teaching interviews.

One thing was sure for the return trip; I would not go back with Mr. Hornblower. I had made other arrangements to go back to Bob Jones University with two girls from Mt. Calvary Church in Elizabethtown. Allissa and I cried as I said goodbye, but we knew that it wouldn't be long for me to finish my finals and make the long trek back before the second semester started in late January. We could make it for two weeks being apart, but after that we thought we would never be apart again.

After attending the evening church service in Elizabethtown, Pastor Terry Smith invited me over to his house for an after service meal and a time of fellowship with some other good friends from the church. Once we were at his place, he presented me with an envelope. He asked me to open it. I was afraid to, dreading what I thought was in it, for that morning in church he had asked me how school was going and how it looked for the spring semester. I told him I was carrying a 4.0 average, but that I was behind on my school bill and would need to sit out the spring semester to pay back my $1000 debt to the school. I opened the envelope, and planned to look surprised, but deep inside me old Jonah knew what it was and that I would not be returning to see Allissa in just two weeks, but that it would be four months before I would cross the Mason/Dixon line again.

When I opened it there were ten fresh one hundred-dollar bills. Pastor Smith had mentioned my financial dilemma to the church choir as it was practicing. They immediately took an offering and raised the $1000. I am still bitter towards that choir. How could they do that to me? I wanted to burn those $100 dollar bills, but I knew it was God's will to continue school, and if I didn't yield then that I would really pay the fare later. I immediately called Allissa from Pastor Smith's. Before I could even tell her the "good" news, she said she knew why I had called and that she had a gut feeling that I would not be returning in two weeks. I said, "Goodbye, I love you! The time will go by fast and we'll be married." Time has gone by fast and this year, marks our twenty-seventh anniversary.

THIS CHAPTER IS DEDICATED to Dr. Bob Jones, III, Pastor Terry Smith, Pastor and Mrs. Keener and to all those at Mt. Calvary Church of Elizabethtown who prayed and paid my way through college as well as to Dr. Custer, Dr. Bell, Dr. Beale, Dr. Schnaiter and my other Bible professors at Bob Jones University who have dedicated their lives to training young preachers. I hope that I will never pull a Jonah and disappoint any of these special friends.

Some of the names in this story as well as in other stories in this book are obviously changed to reduce my time in court. Other than the chapters called Colorado Snow and the Mysteries of the Parco Inn these are all true stories.

CHAPTER SIX

THE "PEACEFUL" VACATION

W e were all looking forward to our annual trip north to see our family and to enjoy the relaxation of a peaceful vacation. I was especially counting the days to get to my mother and stepfather's farm where we could go fishing in their pond as well as just relax and read. I had placed in my briefcase my normal paraphernalia as well as my typical Civil War book, spiritual biography, and this time a book that one of the boys on my T-Ball team gave me for being his coach, called **Comeback.** It was written by Joshua Roh's Uncle Dave, a former professional baseball player who played for the San Francisco Giants. I was extremely interested in digging into that for fun. I thought of bringing some more books, but I knew if I completed those, I could easily pick up another Civil War book at one of the battle-fields we planned to visit.

Prior to our trip, I needed to make sure the van was in good running order. Fortunately, we found that the left rear tire was showing its belts before we left. Unfortunately, it left us with somewhat less money to take on our trip. After further inspection another new tire was purchased, a front-end aligned, a water-pump replaced, a radiator leak fixed and all new hoses put on the van, we were left with no money for the trip, but the blessing was if we could go, the van would be in tip-top shape. After I told my wife Allissa that I spent all of our vacation money on the van, it appeared that she was going to need some extra anti-freeze to keep from over heating. There is something psychologically bad about leaving for vacation without any money, but the Lord remarkably provided, by someone in the church designating $300.00 to us just before we were scheduled to leave.

Sunday finally came, the day we were planning to leave and get a head start on our vacation after the evening service. I had meetings most of the afternoon, which left Allissa the entire task of packing and getting the house in order. Why do girls like to leave with the house in perfect order, for no one will see if it is left a wreck? After the evening service I began to complain about my throat being very sore. I had been talking all day long and had been especially busy that week, so I was somewhat worn down. When we got home to make the quick transition from the car to the van I could not move. I just did not have enough steam to move as quickly as my three excited boys, who were beside themselves thinking of the wonderful vacation ahead of them which we had been building up for weeks. I said, "Honey, I am tired, I need to lie down for just a minute to catch my breath." I never do that, so she knew something was up, but she too was exhausted which led to a very unpleasant conversation, which concluded with me saying that she cared more for her vacation than she did for me.

It didn't take me long to realize I wasn't fit to drive the two hours and fifteen minutes to Rock Hill where we had planned to spend the night with the Schmids. I was able to appease the kids with an ice crème cone, but my dear wife I could not propitiate even with the offer of a Blizzard. If you think the ice crème was cold, you haven't seen anything yet. I said kids, "Daddy is too tired, we will leave for vacation in the morning." After my wife killed herself to pack everything up and get the house cleaned, she painfully watched her house turn in to shambles in just minutes and the majority of her packing undone as we looked for toothbrushes, toothpaste, pajamas, etc. in the bottom of each suit case.

Allissa didn't play any games, that night she called the emergency room at the hospital, since our family Dr., John Miller, was on a cruise in Alaska with our family nurse, Valerie Miller, and asked if she could bring in her sick husband. I don't know if she was calling my bluff or if my pouting and baby act prompted her to think I was dying. I don't know, but she meant business. I told her I was too tired to go anywhere and that I certainly was not going to go to any hospital at 11:00 p.m. She did, however, get me to agree to go to the doctor's the next morning. I said yes hoping she would forget in the morning and that we could get on with our trip.

The next morning all that was missing was the license plate number of the Mac Truck that must have run over me while I tossed and turned all night. My throat was killing me, I had the chilly-willies and to top it all off my neck had the meanest crick in it that I had ever experienced. I was hoping that the only correlation between my sore throat and aching neck was the pillow we had recently purchased on sale. I could hardly turn my neck in any direction and felt that I could be a stand-in for a Frankenstein movie. The boys awoke and jumped on our bed to get me moving. I screamed, but with my throat so sore, it sounded like a muffled, red lobster. With their every bounce, I felt that my neck was going to snap. I told the boys that I'd better go to the doctor, but that afterwards we would roar off!

After saying AHHHH two or three times, and seeing all the streptococci swimming around in the culture, the Dr. said, "You are not going anywhere today. You need to get some rest." I had to agree with him, but I knew how disappointed my family would be to hear that we would be delayed another day, but hopefully the medicine would kick in and we could skeet first thing on Tuesday. When I got home and explained to the boys that daddy needed to rest and that we would leave tomorrow, they said, "That is OK daddy, we love you more than we love our vacation." Where in the world did they get that line? I tried to rest on the couch and began reading **Comeback**, but could not stay awake.

Tuesday came and the boys came running into our bedroom and jumped into bed asking, "Daddy, how do you feel? Are we going?" I screamed, "My neck!" The boys quietly looked as daddy grimaced. I still had the chilly-willies and my throat still hurt but I was now on Ceclor. "Boys daddy doesn't feel real good." "That's OK, we love you daddy more than we love our vacation." Even Allissa said she loved me more than she did vacation. "Boys we're not going yet, daddy doesn't feel so good." Allissa saw the understanding but disappointed looks on the boys' faces and said let's go get some special donuts. They said, "Yippee!" At 10:00 a.m. the chills and sweats broke. Allissa volunteered to pack and load the van for the second time thinking there was a possibility that we might leave later that day. I said, "Start packing I am feeling a little better."

At 11:00 am on Tuesday we took off to parts unknown. Allissa had to look out the side mirrors for me because my neck was still very stiff, but other than that, we were heading speedily North bound. Our plans now changed were to go as far as we could, but not to overdo it. If we had left earlier that morning we could have targeted Harrisburg, PA, and stayed with Allissa's brother and family, but now we would need to stay in a motel. The boys behaved wonderfully and about 6:00 p.m. began the search for a motel in Virginia off I-81. We were looking for a motel with a pool so the boys could go swimming. I was feeling worse and worse, but continued to say, "Just one more exit boys." I don't know how many times we saw a motel with a pool, but only after we had passed its exit and there is no turning around. After saying, "Just one more exit and we will get off" for who knows how many times we pulled into Allissa's brother's driveway instead. They do not have a pool.

I was wiped out, but at least we didn't have to pay for a motel room. When I crawled into the bed I felt like we were still moving, and when I woke up in the morning probably wished we were still moving. My neck was killing me; if only I had been more careful and had placed my head in one of the major craters in the moon bed, I could have possibly straightened the crick out of it. I wanted to just lie in bed, but the boys were already up and exploring the new territory. Since we did not know the new territory at Les' new place, we felt we'd better get up as well.

The boys were somewhat bothered that we could only stay at Uncle Les' for just an hour before we had to take off again for another three hours of driving. Since we got off to a late start we had to do some extra squeezing to see everyone, and we had to meet my mother at the nursing home to give her a ride back to their farm in New York State as we had previously planned. After Allissa reloaded the van for the third time, we headed east towards Philadelphia where we were going to stay the night at my grandmother's. This would be the first time for us as a family to spend a night there. She had Uncle Jerry set up a pop-up camper for us by the side of the house. Allissa reported to me that the skies were clear, since I could not look up, and that it looked like we were going to break our camping streak of having it rain when we camped out.

We arrived just in time for a wonderful lunch at my grandmother's. Allissa unpacked again because I still was feeling very weak. After several hours of visiting we needed to go to the nursing home, where my grandmother Chips lived. My mother had come down from NY with some friends and was enjoying a visit with her mother. The plans were that we would take my mother back to NY on Thursday. Otherwise she would be without a ride. This was one of the reasons I felt we needed to press on regardless of how I felt. The other reason was that Chips wasn't feeling very well and we wanted to see her. I guess when you are eighty-nine years old you have a right not to feel too spunky.

When we got to the nursing home, we found Chips sleeping and didn't want to wake her. She was doing far worse than what we had thought. After several hours of keeping the kids off wheel chairs, walkers, beds etc. Chips woke up. She had suffered a stroke several months before which left her somewhat confused as well as not being able to speak. We had hoped that she would recognize us. The Lord unusually worked so that she recognized each of us. We each took turns holding her hand and talking with her. As we were leaving, Chips quietly opened her mouth and said, "I love you Robbie."

About dinnertime we left to look for my annual splurge for real hoagies, the ones in the South just don't compare to the hoagies up North. So every year we pig out on huge hoagies. We got to my brother Randie's house with all the smells of an Italian deli. I couldn't wait to dig in. After two bites of my sub, I wanted to say, "Y'all come back, ya hear." What would be the odds of getting a southern sub in PA? The hoagies were terrible! I ate the boys' hoagies and mine anyway. After a short visit with my brother, we had to get on the road again for the hour drive back to my grandmother's. When we arrived at 8:30 p.m. at my grandmother's we found another dinner waiting for us. I couldn't believe it, she had pizza, and to complicate things, Northern hoagies! I could not refuse them despite just eating nearly three hoagies an hour before. Later that night, I truly thought the South was going to Rise Again. After saying good night to my grandparents we all rushed to the camper to escape the down-pour and to zipper up the camper before everything got wet. The camping streak was still alive!

The next morning we had a delightful time visiting with my grandparents and the boys had a wonderful time playing in their fields! I hated to tell the boys we had to pack up for the fourth time and that we had an seven hour drive ahead of us that day. I wanted to visit my father, but time dictated that we would have to catch him when we would come back through. The boys enjoyed picking the ticks off their legs and placing them on the carpet floor of the van.

That morning we went to the funeral home in Downingtown to assist mom in the plans for a funeral, for we knew Chips was not doing well at all, it could be days or it could be weeks. We then went from there to visit with Chips and then to take my mother home to NY.

Chips was again in a deep sleep. We were so hoping that she would wake so we could have one last special time with her before we went home and before she went home. Finally after four hours of waiting at the nursing home she woke up. She again recognized us. This we knew would be the last time that we would spend with Chips. I picked up each of our boys and held each to Chip's face to kiss and to look into her eyes while telling her that they loved her. She likewise mouthed that she loved them. I prayed with her and then told her it was OK for her to go home now. She had waited to see each of our three boys born and had held each of them as a baby, but now there were no more babies on the way. When I kissed her goodbye, we both knew it was for goodbye. I told her I loved her and then I said,

"Don't let your bananas get black," which I always said to her when we were about to leave. The signal that it was time to leave had always been when her hair began to fall down from her bun. Ironically, that week the beautician had cut her hair the shortest I had ever seen it, so that there was no hair to put up again. Like Samson, her strength was gone.

When it was time to go I sent the family out one by one after they had kissed Chips and said they loved her; then I kissed her, waved good-bye and walked out of the room. Once down the hall and out the exit door, it hit me that I would never see Chips again on this side of heaven. I had left many times before mentally preparing myself that each visit might be the last time that we would see Chips, but this time we all knew this would be the last time. The finger was then pulled from the dike and the floods flowed down my cheeks. I was able to pull myself together by the time I got back to the van and before my mother came out after saying her last good-bye.

It was then 5:30 p.m. everything was on empty but the gas tank, which would carry us the 250 miles needed to get to mom's that night. Again the kids were near flawless, even as we broke the 1,000-mile barrier that night for the trip. We stopped for a snack at a mountain, turkey restaurant where we each had a stale peanut butter fudge Sundae. I guess that's what you should expect when you have a Sundae on a Thursday.

Friday morning, after a heavenly sleep in an old familiar bed at the farm, I felt like I had a new lease on life. The original game plan was to go to Allissa's on Friday and return to the farm on the following Tuesday and remain for the rest of the week. The farm is the only place usually on our trips home where we can get some rest and actually unwind. I could not wait until next Tuesday to finally relax and begin reading *Comeback*, but today we would need to pack up for the fifth time and head the two hours back south to Pennsylvania to visit with Allissa's parents and family.

This was hard for the kids to understand, for we had just gotten there the night before. John was especially disappointed because we had told him when he got to Grampy's, that if he caught a small-mouth bass 18 inches or longer in their pond we would have it mounted for him. We did have enough time to take Mr. Edward's BB gun and kill two and one half pigeons out in the barn. The boys enjoyed the morning at the farm and then off we went.

After arriving at Allissa's place the boys were off and running in the woods, creek, etc. They love it at all of their Grampy's! That night we had a great time with my nephews, Matthew, Ryan and Jason. We played games and ate and ate, my can those three teenagers eat. Bless the future wives of these behemoths. Bless Aunt Audrey and Uncle Jerry!

We made plans for the next day, Saturday July 4th, to go on a fishing trip to three mountain ponds with my nephews. It was exciting to see all of us pull in some sunnies at Big Pond and then to watch the older boys pull in some big-mouth bass as well as some pickles and onions in another mountain pond where we chased away some deer.

We couldn't stay too late fishing, because it was Allissa's birthday and the family had planned a big party. If I was late there would be some real fireworks on this 4th of July. Allissa still was somewhat miffed from the previous year's birthday, when I bought her a fishing rod from Murphy's. That evening, despite being late, we all had a wonderful time at the family party and a great night with the nephews playing games. We were going to go to the fireworks at Jarvis', but I was fried, I had overdone it with the boys, but I wouldn't have done it any differently.

Sunday, a day of rest, after working to find all of our wrinkled Sunday clothes we headed off to church. The trip had been so hectic that we had already missed a prayer meeting service and just hoped the Lord would understand that our ox was in the ditch for most of our trip. I was excited because I would be preaching and all the family would be there at Mosherville Bible Church to hear the message "Why Do Good Fathers Have Bad Sons?" After the message, we headed back to Allissa's for lunch. My three sons asked me if they were bad sons! As we traveled, the fast moving clouds looked ominous, but I didn't give them a second thought as we traveled down the dirt road through Correyland at 12:45 p.m.

After lunch it was decided that we should all pack up in our van and Grampy's camper and travel the three hours north to Syracuse, New York to see Steve, Allissa's brother. We all wanted to see Steve, especially since we hadn't seen his new house, but to be quite honest I wasn't too excited to add another six hours of driving time to the trip. The poor kids! My poor wife! Poor me! I was already dumb; I mean numb from driving. Could we take another big drive? The push was on, I did not want to be the bad guy if we did not go, so I put on the white hat and we took off. I encouraged the boys that Uncle Steve had a swimming pool and that they could go swimming there.

After just missing a terrific hailstorm off the lakes we drove through the rustling of prematurely fallen green leaves and arrived safely in Syracuse. The kids were excited to go swimming in Steve's pool, but ice-skating would have been more appropriate. There were no green leaves in the pool, but I would have felt better if there were. The weather was unusually cool for July, in fact it had dropped to the 40's and 50's at my mother's. Needless to say, you could hear the boys' teeth chattering after the first jump in the pool. So much for swimming, it was too cold. That was just fine, because the pool had reminded me of my throat culture with all the critters swimming in it.

We had a nice cookout and then I thought it would be nice to call my mother to see if she was OK and to tell her where we were just in case she needed to call about any news regarding Chips. My mother answered the phone and in a monotone voice unnatural to her, said "Hello Will, did you get my message on Allissa's parents answering machine?" I said no that we had left and gone to Syracuse. She then went on to say that Chips had died that evening. It came as no surprise because I had a gut feeling that when we left for Syracuse, which would be the most distant point from Chips on our trip, that we would receive word of her death. I also had a hunch that the way this trip was going that we would not have that peaceful vacation at the farm that we all so desperately needed and looked forward to having. I said that I was sorry to hear of Chip's death and that we would take-off in the morning to come back to the Western part of the state to be with her and Grampy Dick.

The next morning, Monday, I jogged for the first time on our trip. My brother-in-law Steve and I ran for a short run of 2 miles, it about killed me. I had lost much ground in just one week by being on the inactive list. Hopefully I could **come back** and run with Steve again and give him a good workout.

After getting cleaned up and before we were to leave for my mother's, I caught a glimpse of the headlines on the newspaper. The headlines read that a tornado had hit Sunday afternoon in Correyland, PA throwing a mobile home some 30 feet in the air. Those ominous clouds we had seen were hiding a tornado. They had tucked away quite a knock out punch, which we missed by just one round. After saying goodbye to everyone and telling them that we hoped to **come back** before another ten years elapsed, we headed west on the New York Turnpike.

That afternoon we arrived, after traveling the scenic route down through the Finger Lakes of New York. Mom was not there, but was shopping. Grampy was in the barn unloading hay into the lofts from the wagons. We threw hay! I didn't know what hurt more, my neck with the crick or my un-calloused hands getting shredded by the bailing twine. Regardless, we were finally at the farm. The view out the barn was beautiful and the breeze so clean and fresh. That night we had a fantastic dinner and a wonderful time together. We talked some about the funeral plans and made calls to the family to see when everyone could get in to Philadelphia for the funeral. It was determined that Thursday would be the best for everyone.

After the second great sleep of the trip, we took it easy for the day and actually did not leave the farm. It would be the only day during the entire vacation that we did not start the engines. Speaking of starting the engines, the van was losing its tailpipe and was gearing up to be a contender in the next Pocono 500. It was really a blessing in disguise, however, because the van had begun to stall at every stop sign or light since Syracuse and with the engine roaring I could hear and keep the idle high enough so that the van could maximize the use of the power steering and power brakes.

It was nice to take it easy. That day all I did was help unload and stack 900+ bales of hay into the barn. My neck was feeling better I thought, but the reason might have been that my back was hurting so much from throwing over two tons of hay around, that it took the focus off my neck. We also spent a good portion of the day fishing for our first ever fish fry at Grampy's and perhaps last. John was so hoping to catch his trophy fish, but was disappointed when he only caught one small perch. I caught five small-mouth bass and was quite pleased with myself! In fact, I actually took several of them off the hook without wearing gloves. Grampy cleaned the fish and I watched; it was pretty repulsive. Next summer I hope to clean the fish all by myself, but for now, I was quite glad to watch Grampy do it. Mom cooked the fish just like our Southern friends at church told me to do it. I am sure it was delicious, but after just watching Grampy clean the fish, I had somewhat lost my appetite and was feeling guilty about their slaughter. I think John was upset too, because he did not eat one bite of the highly promoted fish fry.

The next morning was Wednesday and we needed to make our way south to my grandmother's to make the final preparations for Chip's funeral. I was dreading the seven-hour trip and felt so sorry for the kids. They had been so good and had not complained at all about the excess of driving. Even at their tender ages they seemed to understand that they needed to cooperate and be a support to their parents. John, who was seven, when he had heard that Chips had died, said "Oh No!" Jim, who was five, cried when he heard. Ben, who was two, did not understand. After loading the van up for the eighth time, we roared off!

After two hours of driving we drove up to a long line of traffic. Two tractor-trailers had collided on a metal bridge on Rt. 15. The traffic was backed up for miles. The traffic person must have thought I was being obnoxious as I kept revving my engine up at every 15 feet of progress. Finally we got to the intersection before the bridge where people were being sent in different detours. I screamed out over our engine's roar, "Which way to Williamsport?" She screamed, "Turn left and keep taking rights you can't miss it!" It is a mathematical certainty if you keep taking rights that you will end up at the same spot you started, so with some hesitation, we were off onto the mountain roads that would eventually lead to Williamsport. I was told that there was a short cut on a dirt road that someone's, uncle's brother knew, but I opted for all the rights.

Once in Williamsport we stopped at a very fancy restaurant for lunch where we had prearranged to meet Allissa's parents. There an elderly couple complained that they had taken a short cut, but added one hour to their trip thinking that the car in front of them knew where they were going. Allissa's parents were under the impression that we were going to **come back** up after the funeral to try again to get some rest and peace and asked if we wanted them to watch the kids while we went to the funeral. It was clear that they shared our disappointment that our plans had changed. After the boys finished their Happy Meals we sadly said one last soupy good-bye to Allissa's parents and took off down the road with the boys in tow.

We arrived at my brother's at about 6:00 p.m. He was to give us Chip's wedding band which my mother wanted Chips to wear. However, there was some sort of mix-up and he had not yet picked the ring up from the nursing home. I said we would take care of it even though it meant some backtracking. After arriving at Zerbe Sister's Nursing Home, I asked if anyone would like to go in quickly with me to pick up the ring. All agreed to go with me but Jim, he wanted to stay in the van and color. We said that would be fine. The reality that Chips was gone hit as I walked by her room, I was so hoping that they had not yet moved a new patient in. Thankfully, it was empty. That alone sent tears down my cheeks, but the thought of someone taking her place would have been too much, because no one can take her place. I wanted to envision all the special visits that we had shared in that room and I didn't want the image marred.

We picked up the ring and thanked the nurses for their wonderful care of my grandmother. Joanne, mother's favorite nurse, later said that just before Chips died she extended her frail arms up to heaven. When we got to the van, we found Jim weeping and found out the real reason he wanted to stay in the van was not to color. He said he loved Chips and that he missed her and that he did not want to go into the nursing home because it would hurt his feelings. I think his feelings were already hurt.

Driving in the comforts of our air-conditioned van, which buffered us from the 100+ degree temperature being produced from the summer's worst hot spell; we drove the last hour of the day to my grandmother's where we would camp out again. This time camping we wished it would have rained. Technically our camping rain streak had ended, but it is not official until I meet with a meteorologist to see how many beads of sweat on the ceiling of a pop-up camper are needed to be considered precipitation. What a night!

The next morning, the day of the funeral, we were in a blitzkrieg pace to get prepared. We also did not want to take the van into Philadelphia to the cemetery with the sound level like it was, they have enough complaints with the airport nearby, so we took it to a shop to have it fixed. I guess I should have asked what it would cost, but they were so kind to squeeze me in that I felt kind of sheepish to ask. After an hour, I understood why they squeezed me in. With the new gold-plated exhaust system, my only concern now was that I would not be able to hear the engine and would stall in the stop and go traffic in Philadelphia. I considered asking them to fix the idle problem, but I think they were planning to go on a vacation after they put on my exhaust system.

Anyway, we needed to get quickly to the funeral home to give the funeral director Chip's ring and white gloves. We also felt very responsible to make sure everything was in proper order since no one from our family came to the viewing. Historically, our family does not attend viewings. I was going to accommodate our family's idiosyncrasy but Allissa wanted to say one last good-bye. I conceded and went in with her and the boys. We had huddled to discuss what we were about to see and do. We went to her casket, and saw her peacefully resting in the clothes that Allissa and mom had picked out from her wardrobe on the previous Thursday. The funeral director had done an outstanding job in preparing her for the viewing. She looked twenty years younger. This visit would leave me with the fitting impression of how I would like to remember Chips. She was at peace in perfect beauty and dignity. We all cried and had a word of prayer by her casket. Afterwards I felt so bad that none of our family had seen her, but was so grateful that I gave in to my wife's desire. It would especially help me with my composure at the graveside service.

My other grandmother, Virginia Senn, a long time, thoughtful friend of Chips, wanted to go to the funeral so we needed to scoot back to pick her up before tackling the adventure of the Surekill Expressway. It was a special treat to have my grandmother with us. We arrived early at West Laurel where I had visited thirty-two years before when my grandfather was buried there. Having some extra time we picked up a corsage for my mother and a boutonniere for my Uncle Jim. Back at the cemetery, family and friends began to pull in, with Brother Bruce barreling in at the last minute. It was great to see my three cousins from the Midwest and my Uncle Jim and Aunt Betsy as well as the other twenty or so people there.

I was to moderate the funeral and give the message and Uncle Jim was to give the eulogy. He did an outstanding job and covered much of what I was going to say about Chips which was even more appropriate coming from her stepson. I read and briefly commented on Isaiah 35, which Chips had asked me ten years ago to read for her funeral.

The heat was unbearable even under the shade. That coupled with the fact that no one had any chairs to sit on caused me to streamline my message. I did not know previously why Chips had wanted me to read that portion of Scripture, but providentially the night before, while I was glancing through her Bible, I found that she had recorded in the back of her Bible that Isaiah 35:1 was one of her favorite verses. The blessing was that in my prior preparation I had asked the Lord to show me a verse or passage to use in the funeral. The verse that was impressed upon my heart was Isaiah 35:1. The greatest find, however, in her Bible notes were the words "July 12, 1982, From this day forward, everlastingly forgiven." This she must have written in her Bible after we had clearly presented the gospel to her on one of our many visits. She had written to me in that same year that she had accepted the Lord as her personal Savior and that the Bible had come alive to her. I believe we will see Chips again!

After the funeral, we traveled up the PA Turnpike to my Brother Bruce's house where the family was going to meet and have a special time together. The food was delicious and the short time with my geographically distant relatives was priceless. The boys built a Tee Pee and continued to be model braves. We were so proud of them. We would have liked to have stayed longer, but grandmother was fading and so was her grandson. Despite the 100+ heat we had a good night's sleep.

We had considered going back to New York to extend our vacation as well as to visit my dad who we had not seen on the trip, but deemed it best to head south the next day. On Friday, after a wonderful breakfast at grandmother's we loaded up the van and decided to take a new way home since we were so close to Philadelphia, I-95. The temperature was projected to rise to 110 degrees. Thirty minutes into the trip we believed the weatherman, for the van began to bake inside. The fans were still running, but no cool air was coming from the vents. It did not take us long to recognize that the compressor had frozen up or at least that's what the mechanic later said. Sounds pretty fishy to me, how could any thing freeze up when it's over

100 degrees outside? Anyway, it was hot, and so was I for choosing to go on I-95 through Baltimore and Washington. What a day-mare! Eight lanes of insanity! One advantage to having your windows down is that you can scream at the cars that want to play bumper car with you at 65 MPH. Why can't people just stay in one lane? What's the big rush?

The kids were hot but well behaved. After passing through Richmond, we told the boys we would stop at the battlefield in Petersburg. After wiggling through the city we found the battlefield and timed it perfectly to see them load and fire a canon. The men doing the reenactment were burning up in their wool uniforms. We would like to have stayed longer to study the historical significance of the battle, but it was just too hot and we were so tired.

On the road again, we said, "Boys keep your eyes out for a motel with a swimming pool." After saying, "just one more exit" for who knows how many times we pulled quietly into our driveway at 204 Maple Blvd. It was so great to be home, even though it was late, but at least we did not have to pay for a motel room. We tried to get in to the house, but realized we had lent out our keys for some friends to use our house if they needed a place to stay. The kids were excited to see their dog still alive, but could not believe we were asking them to get in the van one more time so we could run down a key to get into the house. After getting the key and into the house we all collapsed.

The next morning we went out and got some donuts for breakfast and had a special pow-wow where Allissa and I wanted to just praise our children for their behavior and help on the trip. I fought back tears the whole time as we reviewed the 2,500-mile trip. I wanted to do something so special for each of them, but it was clear that their heart's need was being met by mom and dad just being with them and sharing their hearts and love for them. Allissa went grocery shopping that morning and the boys went outside to play with Windsor. As I collapsed on the couch, the whole weight of the trip hit me. I cried uncontrollably, then prayed and then went and picked up the book, *Comeback*, and began to read.

THIS CHAPTER IS DEDICATED to my sister-in-law, Dianne Isbell, to my Uncle, Richard Senn and to my cousin, Debbie Cooke. Dianne underwent surgery on December 9, 1992 to have a large tumor behind her eye removed. My Uncle, Richard Senn, nearly died in the same year, but has been on a COMEBACK. Debbie Cooke died on February 17, 2009 as this book was being published. What a wonderful time I had with my cousin Debbie this past summer and her daughter Jamie, the COMEBACK KID, exploring Cooke's Castle.

CHAPTER SEVEN

TOP COPS AND A LOWLY PREACHER

I t was my day off, Monday, September 7, 1992. It was a beautiful day to mow and to catch up with the maintenance around the house. In the afternoon my wife, Allissa, and our two younger children and I went for a walk on the new lot that we were hoping to close on the next day. We took some liberties to cut down some small pines and to unclog the old spring on the property. After John arrived home from school we prepared ourselves for our first class of Dog Obedience Training at Tri-County Technical College. I was exhausted, but it was enjoyable to have my two older sons sitting next to me in College. We were going to take the class together so that we could better control our golden retriever, Sir Arthur of "Windsor." After the class, we went home to have dinner. I was starved as well as exhausted and couldn't wait to process the kids and just lie down on the couch and watch the idiot box, perhaps watch the first half of the Monday Night Football game before calling it a day.

We had just sat down to dinner when the phone rang. This is nothing new to be interrupted at dinner by the phone. In fact, one individual calls me nightly for advice on dating. He had recently had a disagreement with his girlfriend over Christian standards for dating. He had wanted to guard their relationship from going too far down the physical road, which I could greatly appreciate. He did not see it wise for them to smooch on dates. She, on the other hand, had ardently fought for kissing rights on dates. Their relationship had been strained. Even my counsel to him to kiss and make up had not fully reconciled their riff.

When the phone rang I thought it was just another call on Dating 101. How wrong I was. My wife said it was Sergeant Pruitt of the Oconee Police Force and he needed to speak to me regarding Bertha, a woman the church had helped last year at Christmas time with a temporary housing need. The officer on the phone stated that Bertha had just shot a loaded 38-caliber pistol at her son Rick. I was further informed that Bertha had locked herself inside her house and had warned the police to get off her property or she would shoot them through the windows. She had also called her daughter Belinda and told her that she had swallowed all of the medicine in the house and was going to die from the overdose. Sergeant Pruitt said they were currently at a stalemate, but they had learned from Rick that Bertha had once confided in our church and in me for help. Rick thought she might listen to Pastor Senn. Sergeant Pruitt went on to ask me if I would come to the scene to see if I could talk to her. I agreed immediately.

My wife knew something was up and looked very troubled when I briefly described the phone call. She was not too excited about my going, but knew it was the right thing to do. She also knew that the Lord had protected me once before in a similar situation when I was able to take a loaded gun away from a man who had held off the police and had resisted any help for several hours. Flashbacks of that incident flooded my mind, especially the fear of walking into a quiet house anticipating a blood bath at any turn. It had taken Bert Campbell and I two emotionally draining hours in the previous encounter to convince Mr. Grover to give us the gun and to get him some help. He had sat in front of me for those two hours with the gun pointing to his heart, threatening to "drop the hammer."

After kissing my wife Allissa goodbye, I jumped into the Buick, believing it to be the faster of our two vehicles. Despite the water pump problems, which were causing the car to overheat, I floored old blue and headed to Seneca to the stake out. My adrenaline was flying as I watched the speedometer needle disappear. I took some liberties knowing that if I were picked up for speeding the policeman on duty would certainly understand my hurry and would escort me to the scene. I also knew if Bertha had taken all the medicine she claimed to have taken, one minute could make a big difference. I prayed and asked the Lord to be my Shield and my Protector. Quick thoughts flashed through my mind about what would happen to my three kids and my dear wife if I were shot. I tried not to dwell on those morbid thoughts for too long, but bore down on the road and screeched through the next bend.

It was now getting dark. The house was locked and all the lights were off. Bertha would not answer her phone when her doctor attempted to call, nor would she answer the police whom she had threatened to shoot if they walked on her property. Was she conscious? Was she alive? The police did not want to knock the door down, except as a last resort. It was at this point I arrived at the corner where I had been told to meet Sergeant Pruitt. Along with him were several police cars and an ambulance. After our initial introductions, I asked if they had a game plan. I was somewhat surprised to hear that I was their game plan. They wanted me somehow to position myself so I could speak to her through one of the two cracked windows. I said I would give it a shot. I rode to the house in the unmarked police car with Sergeant Pruitt.

The house and the surrounding area were all new to me. The additional darkness brought on by the many tall trees on the property gave me the heeby gibes. I could hardly see the outline of the house. Once my eyes began to focus, I was able to see a policeman staked at each corner in the back of the house and another policeman sitting safely behind his steering wheel in the side parking lot, smoking a cigarette. It was a strange feeling to see all the policemen stationed and ready to move, yet all noticeably feeling somewhat reserved about who was to make the first move. Bertha had already fired once and had threatened to shoot anyone on the property, which would now include me. The only difference between the policemen and me was that they were wearing bulletproof vests; I had the Lord as my Shield. I would have preferred both.

Sergeant Pruitt and I slowly and quietly worked our way back to the window in her bedroom. I could hear an old, familiar song playing on the radio. I knocked on the window then moved out of the shooting angle and began speaking loudly so she could hear me. I told her it was Pastor Senn and that I was there to help her. I told her how sorry I was to hear about how she was feeling. I told her there was hope and that we wanted to help her. After pleading for what seemed like decades, there was still no answer. Before attempting to scream in through the front window, which was slightly open, we heard her phone ring, and the answering machine go on. She did not answer it. We moved to the front and I repeated my pleas with her to let me in to talk with her, telling her we truly wanted to help. There was no answer. We were all very frustrated! I really thought she would respond to me, which led me to think the worst. It was about this time, I later found out, that Allissa had called a handful of people in the church to pray for me. As a result, God began to respond to their earnest requests. The Lord had been my Shield and now I was hoping He would work in Bertha's heart to let me into the house.

Sergeant Pruitt and I were walking away from the house in frustration, when we realized if her answering machine was working, I could get a message to her over the phone. We quickly went to the home of an unsuspecting neighbor who was oblivious to the fact that there were at least six troopers in his neighborhood. He immediately let us in and allowed me to make the phone call over to Bertha's house. The phone rang several times before the answering machine came on. This was one time I was glad to get an answering machine; maybe there is hope for them after all. I spoke as loudly and as clearly as I could, and told Bertha that I was at a neighbor's house and in just a few minutes I was going to come over to knock on the front door and that I was coming in. I asked her please to let me in the house. I hung up and we returned to the front of the house.

The officer on the backside of the house said he heard my message, loud and clear. If she were alive, there was no way she could have missed the intention of my call. I was coming in. I knocked on the side of the house to see whether she would respond, to our surprise she did, gruffly, and told us all to hit the road and get off her property. Finally, something! We knew she was alive, but she sounded scared and confused. I tried to keep her talking but to no avail. She wanted the police out. I said, "Bertha, would you let me in if I send all the policemen off the property onto the road so you can see that I am alone?" She said yes. I immediately asked all the officers I could see, to move to the street, away from the house. Sergeant Pruitt, before departing for the road, said, "Are you sure you want to do this?" I didn't think that I really had any other option and said, "Yes." He looked concerned but smiled when I screamed in to Bertha and said, "Bertha, I am coming in now so please put the gun down. I know you might not be a good shot, but, as you know I am an awfully big target." (200+ pounds stretched out over a 6 foot, 4 inch frame.)

Once the police were out of the way, Bertha turned on the kitchen light and I went to the front door. She slowly cracked the door and there, staring me in the face, was a very dazed woman with a 38-caliber pistol. I tried to keep her talking, but was at a loss for words.

I tried to open the screen door, but it was wedged in tight. There I was a sitting duck, trying to open the stupid door while a highly distraught lady pointed a loaded gun at me. All of a sudden there was a loud bang! It was the screen door finally coming open. I walked in and asked if we could sit down. She said yes. I had to clear off a chair to sit on, but was finally able to talk with her. I knew if I could get the gun away from her the danger would be over, so I told her that guns made me nervous. Knowing it was her last tangible piece of security, I asked if she would put it on the table. She did, slowly I reached for it and put it on the other side of the table on a chair, then breathed a sigh of relief. Now if the police would just be patient and let me try to console her and get to the root of her problems.

After listening to the many pressures she faced, innumerable physical problems, a son-in-law feud, a bout with her teenage son, and financial setbacks, it was obvious she was going to need more help than we could provide. She needed medical help to get her blood and sugar levels regulated, and she needed a place to stay where she could be kept from harming herself or others. I was able to convince her of her needs, and that I needed to ask the police to come in to assist. She agreed. They came in, confiscated her gun and escorted her to where she would ultimately get some temporary help. Sergeant Pruitt and all the policemen shook my hand and said they couldn't have done it without me. I told them, "You're welcome," but I knew in my heart it was the Lord Who was my Shield.

THIS CHAPTER IS DEDICATED to the Lord for His faithful watch care over me. Many times I have felt that I was just one step between life and death. I am especially thankful that the Lord saw fit to keep the door closed during the days that I was not prepared to enter into eternity. I now know that I can walk through that door at anytime and find myself in the presence of God because of His grace.

CHAPTER EIGHT

WINDSOR'S NIGHT IN JAIL

ELLO! My name is Windsor. My full-fledged name is Sir Arthur of Windsor. I am a golden retriever of royal stock. My father's name was Sir Buckaroo, hence the "Sir." My father's master's name was Arthur (Art) Johns, hence "Arthur." My friends in the castle call me Sir Arthur, but my master's three boys call me "Windsor." You see the boys have a special grandmother and grandfather who have two golden retrievers for pets, one of which is called London. When I was a little puppy the boys wanted to call me London, but the master said it would be inappropriate since there was already a London in the family. So to be carefully associated with my British ancestor London, the family decided to call me Windsor, or officially Sir Arthur of Windsor.

It was this time last year in December of 1991, when I was born, one of six puppies in the litter. I loved my surroundings in the Johns' house. They kept my nursery room warm and cuddled me each day. I loved to play with my little brothers and sisters. We would fight occasionally, but being the heaviest they soon learned that I would assume the chief seat in the house when it came to feeding time with mamma. Those were special days, dog days indeed. All I would do each day was eat, drink and sleep.

We were all getting bigger. In fact, our masters the Johns were somewhat upset with some of our habits in the house. We of course had not yet been potty-trained and were wearing newspapers for our disposable diapers. Boy did it stink in that room. Then our master used those same diapers to put an ad in them to make our availability known to interested families. I did not understand why they were doing this. All I knew was that we often had strange people looking at each of us and lifting each of us up and asking if we were a boy or a girl. That was somewhat embarrassing for each of us. One day my brother was missing. I wondered where he went. That night I heard my master speaking on the phone explaining to someone how many dogs he had left and that he had just sold one puppy to a family in Easley. I couldn't believe my droopy ears. They were going to get rid of us all. In fact, people were going to buy us. It almost sounded like slavery, how could they put a monetary price on such a royal creature?

The day came in January when some big guy came into our house with some short girl who smiled a lot. However, she looked somewhat apprehensive when she saw all of my brothers and me chewing up everything in sight. The big guy looked at each of us very carefully and then said to the lady, "what do you think of this one." She looked me straight in the eyes, she was hooked, but who could blame her for liking such an adorable charming creature.

It was love at first sight. She also asked, "How big will this dog get?" The big guy said, "Don't worry about that, he's so cute and clumsy." Clumsy, how dare he call me that, what if I called him fatso or fat-head, would he like that? Again, not much respect was paid to me. Do you think they asked me if I liked them? Then to top it off they had three boys. The one little boy picked me up and when I tried to squirm away, he dropped me on my head. The other two boys looked relatively harmless, but you never know, for I had heard horror stories from my daddy Buckaroo that there are some boys who throw rocks and stones at dogs and are very mean. Would these boys take care of me? It sounded like they would, because they were all begging mom to take me home, and each was promising to be nice to me as well as to feed me everyday. In fact, the big guy said to the little lady that she would never have to feed me at all. It sounded very convincing too, but I think I would rather eat her cooking than his.

Finally it was settled. I was the one for the Senn family. They had a big blue moving room to take me home in and a little box to carry me on the trip. This was quite a new experience for me. I hardly had a chance to say goodbye to mom and to big Buckaroo and my little brothers and sisters. I felt very sad about leaving the only world and family I knew. Also the special meals Mrs. Johns made me were just delicious, especially with the extra eggs she added to the menu.

I noticed that their oldest boy, John, picked up on one of the mixed emotions of the moment. He was identifying with my emptiness and was asking his parents questions. One question was if I was missing my mom and family. Boy are they stupid! Do you think they asked me how I felt? No way, instead they thought they had all the answers and insulted my intelligence in the process by saying dogs forget about their parents as soon as they have a new home. Just for the record, I have not forgotten my mom and dad and my brothers and yes, I am happy with my new home and family, but I can't forget my roots. I liked that big boy already. He had feelings! I also liked that middle-sized peewee, called Jimbo, he was really sweet. Now the little two-year-old was a different story. I was petrified of him. He had already dropped me on my head, and tried to squeeze the Alpo out of me on the way home in the moving box. I could tell I would have to watch out for him, he looked quite dangerous.

After we arrived at my new home, I could tell I was going to like my new surroundings. They had a big back yard and all kinds of new toys and balls to play with. This was going to be my kind of family. Oops. OUCH! The two-year-old, Ben just sat on me. This is going to have to stop. I was glad that his mother told him to stop sitting on "Windsor." I wanted to say, "Get the kid a horse or a pony, but please lady, I'm not going to be the kid's High Ho Silver," but I refrained my bark. That night there was a big fight about whose bed I would sleep in. John wanted me with him, but there was no way I was going way up there on top of that bunk, and there was no way I was going to sleep with that wiggle worm Ben, so I was relieved when they just let me sleep on the floor. I was exhausted, but finally after all the fuss, the boys and I fell asleep.

It wasn't long and my master's wife was talking about me or her husband living outside if I continued to soil the rugs in the house. Good night! What do you expect from a puppy? The clincher was when the Senn's were going to get a new rug. In fact, I have never seen that rug, because from that day forward I have been relegated to the outdoors. I loved sleeping in the house and felt so much a part of the family, but now you can see where I rate.

Fortunately, the boy with the feelings argued the case for me to have a doghouse of my very own which he wanted to call Windsor's castle. The master, who was no master carpenter, said he would make it himself in the design of a castle. Let's say his intentions were good, but it is no castle and there is some question if it is a real doghouse.

Extra precaution had been taken in its construction and especially in its painting. I overheard the master tell the story of how Jimbo had swallowed the paint thinner when the previous doghouse was made and painted. Evidently he hallucinated all night and was taken to the hospital and could have very easily died. I am glad he didn't, because he is my pal.

This story, however, about a previous doghouse opened up a can of worms for me which would probably taste a little bit like the K-Mart brand of dog food they were now feeding me. How would they like it if they did their grocery shopping at K-Mart? Again, an indicator to where I rate.

I was very curious to hear about this former doghouse. Did they have a dog before and if so, what happened to him? A neighboring poodle later told me the story. Needless to say I was shocked to hear what happened. Evidently, the boys' grandfather had picked the boys up a dog and had brought it to them as a gift. The dog's name was Coo-Ceau. What an idiotic name for a dog. Well, evidently the dog lived up to its name and the master's wife ended up saying, "Either that dog goes, or I go." The story continues that the day Benjamin was brought home from the hospital that the master took the dog to the ... pound! I now knew why I thought that Benjamin was dangerous. He had a long history of dog abuse problems even from his birth. I thought of calling DSS, (Dogs Social Services) to get more details of my rights. I couldn't believe that they would take their dog Coo-Ceau to the pound. How cruel! What's the difference between that and the practices performed at the Planned Pooch-hood clinics?

I heard all kinds of terrible stories as a little puppy from my mother regarding the things they do to dogs in the pound. In fact, I heard they were like the Nazi's in WW II, in that if no one claims you as a pet, it was off to the gas chambers. There should be some law about that! How indogmane! I would certainly have to be careful, because I did not want to go the way of Coo-Ceau. It sounded like old Coo-Ceau was a real barker and that he chewed up everything in the backyard including the clothes on the clothesline.

I didn't like my new "castle," too small and confining. I'm going to grow you know. I'm not a Chihuahua. Plus the bozo had too many nails sticking through it, plus where was the air conditioning system? Someone had told me, I think it was a Collie from Fort Mills, that all preachers had for their dog an air-conditioned doghouse. Boy was I disappointed! In fact, I have protested the dog house ever since and have purposed to sleep next to the house curled up under the bushes and the overhang of the house. Besides, it is much drier there than in that doghouse. The doghouse brings new meaning to the proverbial saying that it's raining cats and dogs. This protects me from what?

It wasn't long after the doghouse was put up that the master's wife was complaining about how big I was getting. She said I had total control of the backyard and that I had prevented her from using the backyard since I would always jump on her when she came out. There was also some complaint about land minds.

This was a real problem, plus they did not like the old fence around half of the back yard, which I had eyed up and had on occasion slipped through. They always seemed to catch me. Each time I got out, I thought that there seemed to be so much more to life than a semi-fenced backyard. One day several men came into the back yard and put up a new chain-link fence around half the yard as well as a special fence around my doghouse. The master watched his new fence go up with glee, but the Mrs. I could tell was not so pleased. In fact, she made it quite clear that the $675 for the fence could have purchased that bedroom suite that she was hoping that the master would get her before she was placed in a nursing home. I laughed; she certainly had a way with words.

I anticipated next a moat around my new kennel. After the kennel, I thought, what next, a chain? Please, not the chain! I don't like kennels, but it sure beats the chain. My neighbor Snowball seemed content with her kennel, but was slightly jealous of the liberties and attention given to me in my backyard. However, one of my neighbors is on the chain and does he hate it. That poor fellow is always getting wrapped up in the chain, always being tantalized by critters that come just within inches of his run. I am thankful that they don't put me in my kennel too often, except for when they have guests or some special work to do in the backyard. I don't like it when I'm penned up and I make it very clear to all in the neighborhood that I don't like those arrangements. My master says, "Shut-up" a lot when I'm in my cage and will attempt to threaten me by throwing pine cones. I have feelings too you know and am tempted by such threats to pine away. The boys always stand up for me, however, and say, "Daddy, it's not nice to say shut up!"

My favorite thing to do is to play with the boys in the backyard and to chase all the things they throw for me to fetch. My next favorite thing is to go jogging with my master. He doesn't take me out as often as I would like, but when we do go it is always a wonderful time, especially when we go to the horticulture gardens and he lets me off my leash. Then I can really run and have fun. You see, my master, when he jogs, is a very slow runner. One man has appropriately identified him and his running buddies as misplaced sea turtles.

All was going well, but then things began to pile up, my master was furious that I jumped up on him with dirty paws and stained his new suit, the Mrs. was upset that I was barking so much, and again the dangerous one was continually being a tattle tail and saying to the Mrs. that I knocked him down. In fact, he even said, "I hate Windsor." What do you think of that coming from a Christian family? Hate has no place in a home! They just seemed not to understand me. I was just having fun. I didn't mean to hurt the little munchkin, although he is fun to nibble on a little bit. The Mrs. also was complaining more than ever that she was feeding the dog and had been asking where all her promised help to feed Windsor was. The boys, although I think they loved me complained every time they were asked to feed me. How do you think that makes me feel? I didn't want to be a burden on anyone. In fact, I would rather just help myself to their table and feed myself.

As you can tell, things were building up inside. The master wasn't taking me jogging as much as I wanted him to, the boys weren't feeding me, and the Mrs. was upset with me because of the rugs and pillows I had eaten from the clothesline. Then to top it all off, two dramatic things took place in my life and it looked like a third would imminently take place. There was some talk about me going to the Dog Dr.'s and getting my shots. Every dog dreads that and if wasn't for our motto, "Remember old Yeller" none of us would go to get poked at by the Vet. They were all discussing some things that I thought were quite personal. I thought I should have some say in these matters, especially the questions dealing with my manhood.

The day came when I had to get my shots. They treated me first like some animal at the doctor's office. Ouch did it hurt. Again, the wise guy said to the boy with feelings that Windsor wouldn't even feel the needle. The good thing is the kid didn't believe him. Good for you kid. Of course it hurts me. How does it feel when you get a shot? Do you like it? This was about all I could take, but to top it all off my former master signed me up for a dog obedience class. Wasn't that nice? I didn't need school. I'm no Seeing Eye dog. I'm no Lassie! I didn't need to learn any new tricks to impress the neighbors or Grandmother Lee. Please don't take me wrong, I'm no junkyard dog, but isn't this education thing going a little bit too far? Again did I have any say in this decision? I think you are getting the point that by now I needed a little more breathing room. I was seeking my independence. They're not going to tell me what to do!

My first day at Tri-County Technical College was a real eye opener. It's not every day that you can make the big jump from K-9 to College, regardless; here I was with ten other dogs and their masters. I enjoyed meeting some new friends very

Windsor's Night In Jail

much. There was a beautiful, sleek looking gal who used to race in Florida. I had heard from my mother about those Greyhounds who lived in the fast lane and was taught to avoid them. Would you believe it, we had so much in common. In fact, her adopted brother was called Windsor. I thought that I was the only Windsor in the whole wide, world. I was somewhat judgmental of the black lab who thought he was a real cool dog wearing his red collar and red bandanna, but later came to realize it was his master that was the problem not him and he didn't like dressing up either. The German Rottweiler was a real grump, a sauerkraut and wasn't very friendly, far too militant for my taste. Each dog had their own personality, but sad to say there was not one other golden retriever in the crowd, maybe there would be one in grad school.

Our teacher was Mrs. Wang. I thought she was to teach us, but instead it was more like a People's Obedience School than a Dog's Obedience School. I had fun for awhile, but there were far too many distractions for me to listen to my master. He kept yanking the metal leash and was later informed he would need another type of leash to have more success training his dog. School was OK until Mrs. Wang had to let a Border Collie out of the back of her car to use as the example for the class. You should have seen that Collie show off, absolutely disgusting. I can't stand such ostentatious displays of self-righteousness. She thought she was pretty hot stuff, a real hot dog, as she flawlessly obeyed every command of her master. She may have impressed all the masters, but we canines were not moved with her showmanship.

My master and I worked hard during the next few weeks of school. In fact, I humored him on several occasions and gave him the impression that he had good control over me. Boy did I let him fall flat on his face when it was his turn on the final class to go through all the commands with me in front of the whole class. I almost didn't obey any of his commands until I overheard one of the dogs saying, "That golden is really a stupid dog, isn't he?" That did it for me. I then sat on command, stayed on command and came on command. That showed them a thing or two, I'm no dope, nor am I a heel. After class, each master was given a certificate that they had completed the obedience school. Again a great omission, what about me?

Then there was the party, my master prayed before they began eating their pizza and then each of us dogs got a dog bone from the instructor. Now you ask me what would you prefer a piece of Pepperoni Pizza or some old bone that tastes like cardboard? I didn't use the best of manners, but I love pizza, so I licked the plates of several of the masters and tried my best to eat a piece of the turtle, chocolate cheese-cake which I was able to do with great success. Hey, it was my party too! Once again, my master was not pleased with my behavior. I feel like I can never please him. In fact, I don't feel like I can please anyone. No one seems to understand.

After graduation, I felt like I should be able to see more of the world. I was no little kid, but a graduate, and I didn't want to be treated like a little puppy anymore. After being ignored for several days by the family, I tried to get everyone's attention that I had just about enough of this backyard life. I wanted to see the world, or at least my neighborhood. I had to get out.

I felt like my master was putting undue pressures on me. It appeared he did not trust me because he always kept the gates closed around the back yard. Enough of being treated like a dog. I began to bang the double gate by the trash can. I knew if I could hit it hard enough that it would bend just enough so I could squeeze out and get my freedom. The grass truly looked greener on the other side of the fence. After fifteen minutes of banging, a hole was made large enough for me to squeeze through. Just in time too, because I knew my master would be home for lunch in just a few minutes.

Fortunately, I could exercise my rights and live the way I wanted to for a change. I ran down Maple Boulevard and began my jaunt down Holly Street. It was down that street that there were several cute Schnauzers who I could often hear singing their blues in their backyard kennel. Maybe I could visit them and show them that I was no longer a little boy, but a man dog.

I was really enjoying my new found freedom and couldn't wait to impress my friends, when all of a sudden I looked up and there was a car coming my way. My master had warned me many times to look out for cars. He had struck a wholesome fear in my heart with old war stories of his cat Floppy who was flopped by a car as well as their Dalmatian puppy, Shamona, who had been severely torn up in a car accident. I would listen, but I knew they couldn't hurt me.

This car looked a little different than most of the other cars I had seen before. In fact, it was quite curious looking because of all the lights on the top. Then I realized it, I was caught. Who told on me, was it our neighbors? I don't know, but what would be the odds of a policeman going through our neighborhood at this time of day and at the very moment after I had made my great escape. He had me. I hoped he would take it easy on me since it was my first offence. He put me in the back seat behind the metal barrier. To complicate matters I had no dog tags and I am sure he noticed I was underage and that I hadn't been recently inspected. What bothered him the most was my violation of the leash laws in Clemson and that I was roaming the neighborhood without my master. At this point, he did not know who my master was. He only had one option, and that was to take me to Dog Jail. How embarrassing! I hope the Schnauzers don't see me!

Once in dog jail, I felt so guilty. Here I was with hardened criminals, dogs that roamed the streets at night eating out of garbage cans and spreading trash all over yards. There was one dog there who had severely bitten a young boy, another whose joyride in life was to chase cars. There were others there who were just the victims of poor circumstances. One puppy was dropped off in front of a farm when he was a little fellow, and the dog next to him was a dog that was mistreated by his master. There were nineteen of us behind bars that night or was it day, for we really couldn't tell because the jail was totally in darkness except for one dim light that was left on.

I overheard some of the dogs talking despite the whining and barking of the young, homesick dogs. They were saying that tomorrow afternoon they were all heading up the river to Pickens. Pickens is the Alcatraz of the East. That was only one stop away from the gas chamber if no one claimed us. I was starting to cry myself and panic. Would my master find me? Would he forgive me? I was somewhat skeptical that they would be able to trace me especially when the policeman turned in the report stating that I was an Irish Setter. The lady at the dispatch desk didn't seem to know any better either. At least they had it right that at I was "at large," and not recorded as some small dog. He also complained about how much of his time that week had been spent picking up stray dogs. He wasn't ugly, but he wasn't going to win any FHA awards.

That night as I tried to sleep I began to think about how special my master truly was and how fortunate I was to have three little boys to play with as well as the Mrs. who despite her occasional shortness with me had also showed great love towards me. It was then that I came to myself and realized I was wrong in running away from home. My master did care for me and more than ever I realized that the restraints that he had put on me were really for my best interests. Oh, how I wished they would find me.

The next morning a man came by and filled my water jar and gave me some jailhouse dog food. There were certainly no thrills, and most definitely no bowls of excess milk and cereal like I had been accustomed to having at my master's. He slammed the door shut after feeding us all and then locked the door behind him.

Several hours passed, when suddenly the door opened again and light flooded the dark room. Immediately I saw the Mrs. and the dangerous two-year-old looking into my cell. I couldn't believe it, how did they find me? The Mrs. thanked the policeman profusely and I jumped in the back of the car promising to myself that I would never run away from home again. There is no place like home. There is no place like home. There is no place like home.

When we pulled into the driveway, Miss Karen and the Mrs. led me carefully out of the car. They had come to my rescue without telling the master the good news. I had no idea that he would be broken up over my disappearance. I jumped out, and there to my delight was my master. I wondered how he would receive me. Would he forgive me? Would he welcome home, his prodigal dog? The answer came immediately, when he said, "Windsor where have you been? We missed you so badly; in fact I could hardly sleep last night. The boys prayed for you Windsor and asked the Lord to do a miracle especially after they had ridden their bikes through several neighborhoods calling out your name at every other house. Wait till Jim and John see you! Windsor, the boys prayed for you last night at prayer meeting and in fact John tried to merit extra favor by singing a solo for the first time ever in children's choir. He then woke up this morning at 5:35 a.m. and ran outside to see if you had returned. When he saw that you hadn't he climbed up into Jim's upper bunk and woke him up and said, "Jim wake up we have to have a prayer meeting and ask the Lord to let Windsor come home."

I felt terrible to cause the family so much anxiety. I wagged my tail of all the past and determined to be the master's best friend. I still felt bad when the Mrs. broke the news that we had a court date in Clemson and a subsequent fine to pay. I sure hope that they will show grace especially since this was my first offence. The master's joy abruptly turned to anger when he saw me jumping up on the clothesline, and pulling down each of the pillows from the couch. I guess I was just excited to be home. I had better be careful though, because I don't want to go to the pound like poor old Coo-Ceau.

Well I have learned my lesson that there is no place like home and that the grass is not necessarily greener on the other side of the fence.

THIS CHAPTER IS DEDICATED to Art and Thelma Johns for selling us Windsor at such a special price as well as paying for Dog Obedience School. We have added up what he has cost us in just one year, including the fine, the metal fence, doghouse, shots, food, etc. and it totals over $1,000.00. That's more than my tithe. So no wonder this country is going to the dogs. This chapter is also dedicated to Joshua Milsaps who is a dog's best friend and to London and Chester's masters, Grampy Dick and Grandma Lee who are my favorite animal people in the whole wide world.

CHAPTER NINE

THE SEARCH FOR THE
PERFECT CHRISTMAS TREE

I t is Monday, December 9, 1991. Mondays are my day off, so it's today or next Monday to get our tree up. The goal is set, it will be today, and nothing will impede my promise to the family that we will get our tree up TODAY. Well, almost nothing, after being somewhat delayed (three hours) while shopping for gifts with my oldest son John; we arrived home at 5:00 p.m. It didn't help that I locked my keys in the car at the Mall.

It has been our family's tradition to enjoy a quiet, scenic trip to the Christmas Tree Farm at the base of the Blue Ridge Mountains. After explaining our tardiness to my wife, I said, "Kids load up in the van, we are going to get our tree." "Isn't it too late?" says my wife Allissa between coughs as she gave outward expression to her internal bronchitis. "No, get in the van! Yes I know Ben's sick, but just throw him in the van, he doesn't have to get out, nor does he need to get his shoes on, let's go before it gets too dark." We proceeded to go on our quiet [Cough! Cough! "He hit me!" Cough! Cough! "Get back in your seat and buckle up!" Cough! Cough! "He pinched me!" "Shut up!"] and scenic trip. As I backed out of the driveway I turned the headlights on as well as the windshield wipers for it began to pour. Hopefully it will stop raining by the time we get there, I optimistically thought.

"Yea! We are at the Merry Christmas Tree farm!" "OK kids, you will all need to stay in the van as I go out in the rain and look for the perfect tree. I will point to it and you give me the thumbs up when you think it's the right one." Now there were at least 200 acres of Christmas trees, but in your heart you know that there is just one that is right for you and your family.

This year, despite the rain, I had it in my mind that we would buy a dug tree instead of cutting the sap out of some poor pine. I almost got on the campaign wagon with SAVE THE TREE, but I am too busy as it is to branch out into those matters with my ecological friends. Allissa, hesitatingly but sweetly, said "If you want to get a dug tree that would be fine, although it would not be my first choice." My mind was fixed on a dug tree, which after Christmas would be planted by the side of the house where I had planned to plant three evergreens in the spring. Think of the savings if I could kill two birds with one tree!

"Honey, I found it, it's a beautiful Eastern Pine and its only $35, it's the perfect tree, it has our name written all over it!" After all the kids crowded under an umbrella and inspected it with daddy, it was unanimously agreed upon as the perfect Christmas tree. Now if we could just get it in the van. After several minutes of pushing and shoving and pounding the burlap ball into the desired shape to fit between the seats and bending the branches the tree was in.

The man who helped me load it for some odd reason was not very responsive. My wife later said he could only speak Spanish, for she heard him talk to his boss in Spanish, something about "loco hombre." I wish I had known he couldn't speak English because I could have impressed him with my Spanish and at least said "Fleas in the Navy, Dad!" to him, which is Mexican for Merry Christmas. Oh well, we were off and running now with all three boys pinned in the back of the van with an impenetrable barrier between them and mama. After surviving PINE STORM with the kids for fifteen minutes, I realized that we were going to need a metal bucket to put the tree in. I searched in one place, but they had none. It was getting late. The kids were still pinned in the van, and we hadn't eaten. So home we went!

After dropping off two of the boys, mama, and what was left of the tree at home, John and I went to find the bucket. We went to Ole Norm's Hardware, where they have everything, but always for a price. Sure enough, they had the size bucket we needed for $14.95. I thought it was a little steep for a bucket we would only use once a year, but it was the size we needed for the perfect tree. Besides there was the possibility we could use it as a swimming pool for the kids in the summer if only we could find the right size ladder to climb in and out of it. After explaining to Allissa

86

the steal on the bucket and its many uses, particularly the one in front of us, she sighed as she mentally tallied the $35.00 + $14.95.

Now the fun part, putting the tree up nice and straight, but first I had to get that tree into the bucket without getting a hernia. For some reason the tree did not look so big outside as it glaringly did now in our living room. After wrestling with the tree and pounding the burlap ball, I finally had it in the bucket, now I only needed to rotate it to find its best side. How neat, I thought a pre-decorated tree, oops that's the curtain that got caught in the tree.

After turning the tree 360 degrees several times, I realized that the tree really did not have a best side, except out-side. "We'll make the best of it kids, just be patient!" I screamed. All we need now is some rocks and bricks to stabilize the tree in the bucket and to keep it straight. After strategically putting enough bricks around the base of the tree to build a chimney, the stupid tree would still not stand straight.

The boys were trying to decorate their prized leaning tree, when mom looked at the tree. I had a sneaky suspicion she would probably notice that it wasn't exactly straight and would want it adjusted. Girls are funny that way! After we all stood looking at the tree, I could now see why a dug tree was not Allissa's first choice. I don't know if it was the 11 ½ gallon bucket, or the very leggy appearance of this tree, or the missing in action branches from PINE STORM, but one thing was sure, neither one of us was real happy with "our" decision. To complicate matters Allissa's bronchitis was entrenching itself so she called Dr. Miller, who called her in a prescription. She volunteered to put the kids in their pajamas and run out to Revco to get her medicine while I tried to straighten the tree.

As soon as Allissa pulled out of the driveway my mind began to manipulate a solution to the problem. Why not just cut the tree, and put it in the tree stand, but if I did that there goes my idea of planting the tree by the house after Christmas. It was too hard to digest such a plan knowing I had spent twice as much as I should have for a cut tree. The whole idea of cutting the tree would go against the grain of my original intentions for purchasing a dug tree.

Suddenly, a brainstorm hit me, why don't I drive back to Ole Norm's where I also saw some cedar trees for sale and just buy one, put it in the tree stand inside the big bucket and then plant the other tree outside, all before Allissa comes home. She will never know the difference between a cedar and a pine and she will be just ecstatic to see something straight pointing to the ceiling rather than towards the kitchen.

Colorado Snow

"Kids get in the van! Quick!" "But dad we are in our pajamas!" "Shut up; get in the van we have to hurry before Ole Norm's closes at 8:00 p.m." Leaving our driveway at 7:54 p.m. we arrived at Ole Norm's at 7:58 p.m. I ran in to the empty store and said, "Please don't close!" The man that sold me the bucket looked at me rather oddly, and even more peculiarly when I went to purchase one of their trees because I had previously explained to him I needed a bucket for a dug Christmas tree. "Kids, stay in the van, and I will pick up each of the trees outside in the water puddles, and you tell me which one to keep." All eyes sparkled as the boys watched their crazy dad through the picture window of the van until the perfect tree was decided upon by all. What a blessing! The tree was only $16.95! I wish I could have returned the bucket, but the bricks had altered its shape.

After trying to squeeze the wet tree into the van, I realized that it wasn't going to work without irreparable damage being done. The last thing I would ever want to do is hurt a cut tree, you could kill it if you're not careful. So I thought the next best thing to do was just put it on top of the van and slowly drive home with it resting between the storage rails. However, the man at Ole Norm's insisted on getting some bailing twine and securing it. He had the crazy notion that it could fly off. To humor him I said, "fine." I began to climb up the ladder on our conversion van, when I heard a loud rip! Embarrassed by splitting my Sans-A-Belt pants and being in such a hurry to beat mamma back to the house, I did not take the time to tie my side down, but just looped it around a branch and said thank-you to the man.

I knew I had to drive somewhat slower, but I also knew if I didn't beat Allissa home she might get worried, for I left no note to my whereabouts, and all the kids were in their pajamas when she left. The last thing I needed was for her to call the police or the hospital, or even worse, for her to go out searching for us by following the trail of scattered pine needles that we had left behind. In moments we were on our street and then as we neared our driveway my stomach sank as I saw the blue Buick perched in its parking spot. Well, she will understand.

Allissa met us in the carport with the famous hands-on-the-hip pose. "Hi, honey, I have some good news, the boys and I went out and picked the perfect tree, look, what do you think?" All eyes turned to the top of the van and the piece of bailing string hanging from the rail where the man at Ole Norm's had tied his side down. Horrified at the empty sight, I said, "Allissa, I will be right back, the tree is gone, get the kids inside for they shouldn't be out in their pajamas, especially with Ben being sick!" As I backed up with the van, the string tied to the rail went under the back wheel, something had to give, and this time it wasn't the bailing twine. Oh well, I can fix that broken rail later, I have got to find that tree before someone runs over it. After back tracking only a mile, I found the cedar tree by the side of the road! I was relieved to find it and to calculate that it probably hadn't been driven over more than a few times. Throwing it on the roof of the van, I crept down the road with my right turn signal on. "Oh no, here comes a car behind me, how will I explain this, if it is a policeman. Here it comes its a . . . !"

After arriving home I tried to explain to Allissa my logic for purchasing another tree, especially at the almost give-away price of $16.95. Allissa, sized up the situation and after mentally tallying the $35.00 + $14.95 + $16.95 that I had spent in the search for the "perfect" tree, graciously received her husband (and the checkbook). By 10:00 p.m., on Monday, December 9, we had the "perfect" Christmas tree up just as I had promised. By the way, do you know of anyone who needs an 11 1/2 gallon slightly dented bucket?

THIS CHAPTER IS DEDICATED to my wonderful wife, Allissa and my three boys John, Jim and Benjamin.

CHAPTER TEN

"ALLISSA, GUESS WHO IS COMING FOR CHRISTMAS?"

I t was Saturday, January 11, 1975 and Christmas had come and gone. This would be the first time since fifth grade that I would not be on a school basketball team which required holiday and after-school practices. I had tried out for the team at Downingtown High School and was cut. I had never been cut before in my life, except with a pocketknife when I was in third grade. Tragically, there was no Michael Jordan yet on the scene, who could relate to players like me who were cut from the basketball team in high school. It was a terrible feeling to go to Coach Boyer's office and see the list of the names on the door and to find that my name was not on the list. I truly thought I had made the team despite being out of shape and a very poor showing in the try-outs.

Now with no sports to occupy my time during the winter months I looked for a job to make some money. I had just met Jack Thompson, a fellow classmate who loved to ride motorcycles. Jack mentioned that they needed additional ushers at the Exton Movie Theatre. I couldn't imagine a better job than to watch movies, eat popcorn for free and to get paid for it! After the interview with Miss Bortz, who I think was the former drill sergeant for the Marines, the Rangers, the Navy Seals, the state police and Teddy Roosevelt's Rough Riders, I had other ideas of how my new job would go! Regardless, it was my first real job with a W-2 form and it started off at a whopping $3.25 an hour.

On this Saturday, I had to work from 4:30 p.m. to closing. This left me the morning to sleep in and a little time in the afternoon to goof off before needing to get down the road. I did not know how far I would get down the road that day when I first awoke. It was mid-morning when my buddy Slow Joe called 215-269-4311. He asked if he could come down and shoot some hoops. We would indeed shoot, but not some hoops! I hesitated to say yes, because it seemed that every time that Joe and I got together we got in trouble. This day would be no exception. My family had to do some shopping, so when Joe arrived, there was no one home but us chickens. Joe and I quickly got bored shooting hoops by the barn. It also was literally freezing outside in the Keystone State, so we came inside to do some inside shooting.

When Joe and I began to play the game of Risk, he noticed Randie and Bruce's BB guns that they got for Christmas standing at attention in their bedroom next to the bunk bed. Joe already had disdain for the Red Rider gun because my brother Randie shot at him in anger when we tried to scare him when he was home alone. Boy did he ever get in trouble for pointing a gun at someone! Well, Joe seemed to be intrigued with that BB gun and asked if he could see it. I said, "I don't see why not, no harm in seeing it." Joe then cocked it and asked if he could shoot it at one of Bruce's car models. He persuaded me that he had only cocked it once and that there would not be much force behind the BB. I said, "Why not?" Joe always had some half-cocked idea anyway. This would simply be two of them.

Joe then began systematically to shoot at each of the boys' models in their room. As each model was hit, he laughed harder and harder. Joe was amusing to watch; and he did bring back memories of the shooting gallery on the boardwalk in New Jersey. The only problem was we were not on the boardwalk; in fact, we were not even near Park Place. One more roll of the dice and I was afraid we would be nearer to JAIL – DO NOT PASS GO. Joe seemed to have the monopoly on the gun as he delighted in his TORA-TORA-TORA escapade down Battleship Row.

I then began to shoot sheepishly at the remaining targets with Bruce's BB gun. After each shot, my conscience was ringing. I had wondered on many occasions, if Joe had a conscience anymore or maybe he was one of those people who did not get one because he did not have a father and was living with his grandparents. Anyway, I was feeling somewhat bad and knew that my brothers would try vicariously to kill me through the mediation of my parents. My brothers would often yell or cry, "Will hit me" even when I didn't hit them. They had won a few academy awards in their youth and made the boy in Home Alone look like Shirley Temple when they tried to keep me out of their room. This day I knew the evidence was mounting against me and that I would be in big trouble! I could almost see my brothers screaming and crying when they saw their models shattered. I could then see them smiling as I got spanked. Joe never got spanked! Joe also smiled when I would get in trouble.

Joe began to get bored shooting stationary targets and suggested that we open the window of the second-story, stucco farmhouse and begin to zero in on any moving targets advancing up or down Dowlin Forge Road. I didn't think it was such a good idea, but I was easily enticed to follow Slow Joe in his pursuit of an adventure.

I don't know what I was thinking, but I found myself looking down the barrel of the Crossman as the first moving target came our way. Joe and I both fired, I did my best Rupert Vincent imitation, but Joe was locked in. He screamed, "I hit the windshield and it shattered." The next thing we heard were the tires locking up on the road and the car coming to a screeching halt. I was petrified and wondered if we had injured the driver as well. In seconds, that question was answered as we heard someone pounding on the kitchen door downstairs. I think he was screaming, "Let me in, let me in! Or I will huff and puff and blow your house down!" Our Adamic response was to hide. We both went into my room and locked the door and then hid under my bed. I was shaking; Joe was giggling. I said, "Joe it is not funny, we have really done it now!"

Finally, after what seemed like hours, there was no persistent knocking at the door. We then heard the sound of the wounded car pulling away. "Now what do we do?" We assumed that within minutes the next knock at the door would be either Officer Scotty (who I was getting acquainted with) or my parents. Either of which I did not want to face at this time. It was decision time. We could either be responsible and confess our wrongdoing and accept whatever consequences, or we could run. Within fifteen minutes, we were on Route 30 west.

Joe and I were both a little nervous as we quickly discussed the wisdom of choosing Route 1 over I-95. The overriding consideration for choosing Route 1 was that we assumed that there would be more policemen on the prowl on I-95. Route 1 would be slower, but since I was with Slow Joe it just seemed fitting. Inside the stolen surveyor's wagon, we had thrown some clothes and Joe's 10-speed bicycle. The only money we had was the $100 that Joe was able to steal from his grandfather's secret hiding place. We left no notes as to where we were going. One reason was that neither of us really knew where we were going. We were both very lost before we even began our journey.

Colorado Snow

Before getting out of Pennsylvania, we already needed gas. We wondered, "Would we be recognized as the BB bandits at the Gulf station? Would there be any roadblocks?" We filled up the tank, grabbed a couple of sodas and some Butterscotch Krimpets. Somehow Joe got more than me, but that was OK, it was his grandfather's money and my only contribution to the trip was my parent's surveyor's wagon.

We went through towns such as Bel Air, Towson, and Baltimore. It was now getting dark and we were hungry again. The wagon seemed to be hungrier and was sitting near empty. Once again, we filled up. We stopped at a Kentucky Fried Chicken and again Joe got more than me, but I understood because it was his grandfather's money and I only contributed my parent's surveyor's wagon. It was getting noticeably cooler even as we entered into Virginia that night. I was exhausted and already had been wondering if this was really worth it to get a sun tan. I was having some cognitive dissonance and briefly thought that it would be better to go back home and get something else tanned, but Joe was adamant, Florida was the goal with its sunny beaches.

I suggested that we pull over and get some rest. Slow Joe agreed reluctantly. He had asked me many times if he could drive the vehicle. I knew my folks would not like that, so I had been uncommonly firm in my resolve. However, neither of us could sleep. For me my conscience was ticking so loud that I could not sleep, for Joe I think it was the combination of the 40-degree temperature that had crept into the wagon and the vision of sun bathing on the sunny beaches of Florida. Both of us had no idea how much further we had to Florida and neither of us knew if Daytona Beach was on the Atlantic Ocean or the Pacific Ocean side of Florida. Neither of us could recollect being any further south than Maryland and we did not have a map. Slow Joe said he knew that we had at least Virginia, West Virginia, Alabama, Arkansas, North Dakota and South Carolina to go through before even reaching Georgia and Oregon.

After freezing and failing to sleep we thought it best to drive through the night and at least benefit from the vehicle's heater running. After an hour of driving, I hit the wall. My resistance was also down, as illustrated by my yes to allow Slow Joe to drive. I hit the wall, but Joe would soon hit the barbed-wire fence. Somehow I had fallen asleep with Joe driving. When I awoke, we were in a field. Somehow, Joe had gone between two fence posts. He was trying to get the barbed-wire out from underneath the surveyor's wagon so we could continue. The good news was that if anyone saw us in the field, we could say without too many barbs, that we were doing some early surveying work. I was surveying the damage to the van and Joe was surveying the van for something to eat. Somehow, Joe had some extra food hidden away that I did not know about. It did not look very appetizing for it was squished. I then took the wheel, which was fortunately still connected to the wagon, and continued on south. I was fuming! I could not understand how he could miss the mark by so much. He had driven at least fifty yards off the highway. Joe sat there smiling. In fact, he had the same smile on his face that he had when he was shooting BB's at my brothers' model cars, the difference now was the model was only larger.

The sun never came up on this Sunday, January 12, 1975. It was dark and overcast and it began to rain. Once again, the van needed gas and we were starving. Joe did not offer me any food this time. One reason was that we needed gas for the van and the other reason was that the money was his grandfather's. In fact, he said that it would be better not to get any food and to save what money we had left to get us to Florida. His logic sounded good, but my stomach was not convinced. I had been mentally calculating how much money Joe had left. After we got gas, I knew that this was the last tank of gas we could afford. We were now in North Carolina and we were both hoping that South Carolina would be the next state that we would see.

We were both learning much about our geography as well as history. We were both impressed at how all the Civil War battle sites were fought in National Parks. It made sense to keep the fighting away from the cities. We also were aware that the people were talking somewhat of a foreign language. Occasionally, we could recognize a word, but it sure was unsettling. Slow Joe knew we were in the South because South was now in the name of the state. All I knew, I was some 600 miles from home and that I did not know one soul in South Carolina. We also noticed that when we crossed the state line that it was still raining, and even though it said South, it was still forty degrees outside. South Carolina was very flat and piney, I wondered, "Who would ever want to live in South Carolina?"

It was late in the afternoon, and Joe and I had not said a word for hours. The ice was broken with me notifying Joe that we would probably need gas soon and that I wasn't sure we would have enough gas to make it to Florida. Neither of us knew how large a state Georgia was and how many hours it would take to cross it. We were starving.

Joe said to pull over at the next convenience store. This we did and Joe went to work. Other than just the stolen vehicle we were driving, all that I had previously stolen was a tennis ball and some yellow ducky marshmallow candy at the A&P. I still remember the yellow ducky candy tasting so bad that I threw it out. Now Joe added another memorable food item that I would not be able to eat the rest of my life with any pleasure, the moon pie. I had never heard of or eaten a moon pie before. Slow Joe thought that they were made with cheese since they came from the moon. I wasn't so sure what to think. I didn't think they were from the moon, and they sure didn't taste like they came from the earth and why call it a pie? Thinking of pie reminded me of the wonderful apple pies my mom would often bake. I was hoping she wasn't a wreck from worrying.

I had to put those thoughts quickly behind me because we now faced our next dilemma; how to get our next tank of gas which would get us to our destination. We were falling one tank short of the sunny beaches of Daytona, Florida. Joe was trying to get me to fill up and just pull away from the gas station without paying. I told him that I couldn't do it. His next suggestion was that he would do it. Again, I told him no. Then he compromised and said that if we could find a bucket or a jug that he would fill it up with gas and then run with it to a place where I would be hiding with the getaway vehicle. Now this all started to sound like Bonnie and Clyde type-behavior. I foolishly agreed. The first bucket we saw was on the porch of a poor lady who looked like Aunt Jemima. How did I know what she looked like? Because I got a fool's view of her in the rear mirror when she was screaming, "Come back here boy with my bucket!" Joe thought it was pretty funny. The next obstacle was for Joe to get gas in the big washing bucket and bring it to where I would hide the van. Joe did not want to swish gas on his pants, which I could understand because it would not go well with the KFC grease stains, moon pie crumbs, and the mud stains from the fence episode.

His contingency plan was to siphon gas. He had once seen his grandfather do this when his tractor needed gas and he siphoned gas from his VW. "No big deal," he said. All we needed was a hose. Slow Joe disappeared again and in minutes had a hose. Now all we needed was a source to siphon gas. Our first victim was a jeep in a parking lot. Joe was very kind to let me do the honors. I had no idea how to siphon gas and was somewhat skeptical to think how gas could travel uphill to the wagon in a hose. Joe said just suck on the hose and the gas would come out. It sounded pretty simple, all I had to be was the sucker, in which at this point I was exponentially gaining experience. At first there was no response, and then I hit the jackpot on one enormous effort to raise the gas. The only problem was that it came with such fury that I did not retract my lips in time and swallowed a good mouthful of gas. Joe thought this was hysterical. I thought I would die, but not laughing. I smelled like a gas pump and was fearful of creating any sparks for fear of becoming the next zephyr blimp to explode. Fortunately, it was still raining. We decided to find a place to park, get some sleep and regroup in the morning.

We slept very poorly, and it was still raining. I smelled like gas and all I could taste was gas. Joe needed a shower badly. He had enough crude oil accrued in his bleached blond hair to get us to Florida but I did not know how to make the conversion to gasoline. Joe seemed to never lack for schemes. His new plan was to steal something and get money for it at a pawnshop. I had suggested that we pawn off his Schwinn ten-speed bicycle. He strongly resisted that idea. Near to where we stayed for the night was a large textile plant with many cars in the parking lot. Joe began to go through the parking lot checking doors. He then found one that was open which had several bowling balls and a pair of bowling shoes sitting in the back seat. My conscience would not spare me on this transaction. In fact, at every strike on this infamous trip it registered loud and clearly: guilty, guilty, guilty.

My conscience was bowling me over with my need of forgiveness! After finding a pawnshop which was another first for me, we were back on the road again with $20.00 in our hands.

Miles later, we saw our first sign for Florida. It said Jacksonville, Florida 60 miles! We were now only an hour away from the sunny beaches and the quaint little town of Jacksonville. However, it was still raining and it was all of forty-two degrees outside. It did not look like we were going to get a sun tan this day!

Reality was beginning to set in! This was a stupid idea to come to Florida! There were no sunny beaches! Joe, who had been undaunted to this point, began to realize that the beaches would be closed to sun bathing but wanted to continue to drive until there was sun on some beach.

In my heart, I knew we were doing wrong. I also knew that I wanted to go home. I was hungry, stinky, and missing home. There is no place like home. There is no place like home. There is no place like home. After saying that three times in Georgia I found myself still in Georgia. The only reason I could think of was that I wanted to go home to Pennsylvania and not to Kansas. Apparently, I had my wires mixed. So I tried again, "There is no one like mom. There is no one like mom. There is no one like mom." After opening my eyes, I realized this was not a bad dream, but that I was still in Georgia, oh my! I then said to Joe firmly, "We are going back home!" He argued that we were so close to the destination. "Please take me to Florida," he pleaded. I said, "Not on this trip, we are going home." I told him, "If you want to go to Florida you can get out right now and ride your bicycle the remainder of the way, but for me I am going home." I thought this to be only right since my contribution was my parent's surveyor's wagon. Just as I had repented in my heart, I immediately turned the wagon around and pointed her north. I told Joe that I could not steal anymore and that we would somehow get home the honest way.

The van once again was nearing empty as we retraced our steps in Georgia. I pulled into an Exxon gas station in Waynesboro, Georgia to see if I could talk the owner into loaning me $20.00 for gas and food. I determined it would be a loan which I would pay back when I got home. It was late in the afternoon and getting dark. I went into the station and looked for a worker. In the shop a man was working on a car. After introducing myself to him, I found out that he was the owner. I went on to tell him our difficulty and how we had run away from home. I explained to him that we would like to borrow some money, which we would pay back. He looked at my long hair, my pimples, my dirty clothes and the unlikely-hood of ever seeing Andrew Jackson again, and hesitated.

At that time, his wife happened to come to the store. She looked at us with the eyes of a mother; she saw no long hair, no pimples, no dirty clothes, but two boys who needed to go home. She also saw beyond the needs of gas and food, and the broken and worried hearts of parents. She saw two boys far from a heavenly Father as well. She graciously encouraged her husband to give the prodigal sons the loan. With some reservation, he agreed that it would be the Christian thing to do. This was the first bit of sunlight we had seen on our trip!

She encouraged us to call our parents because they would want to know where we were. I agreed. I then dialed 0-215-269-4311 and Joe would call 0-215-269-0507. As soon as my mother answered the phone I started to cry. I did not care what Joe thought as he observed my apparent weakness. My mother also cried and said she was a wreck with worry. She also quickly told me that the man whose windshield we shot had dropped charges and felt terrible that we had run away. Even Miss Bortz, at the Exton Theatre, was concerned and had been calling to see if we were OK. She had hit the jackpot when she told my mother that if she were a gambling woman, she would guess that we were en route to Florida.

My mother then made arrangements to send us money through Western Union so that we could spend that Monday night in a motel, get a decent meal and have sufficient money to come home. (She wisely sent the money to a Western Union just ahead of us in North Carolina.) That night Joe and I slept in a heated motel on a full stomach. Even after a good hot shower I still could smell and taste a little bit of the gas. The next day Joe and I would make the entire trek home. The last four hours the rain had turned to a terrible snowstorm, but finally at 4:00 a.m. I dropped Slow Joe off on the top of Cemetery Hill after sliding and spinning up most of it. From Joe's mother's apartment, I drove down the back roads to home. Dowlin Forge Road looked like a winter wonderland. Everything was as white as snow, well almost everything! (What was not white as snow - my heart, would be, but not until four years later.)

ALMOST FIFTEEN YEARS LATER

IT WAS DECEMBER 22, 1989. The phone rang. On the other end of the phone was a familiar voice, saying, "Do you know who this is?" I always am amused when asked that question, but not on this occasion, it was the voice of an old friend, Slow Joe. Joe had called a month earlier breaking a ten-year period in which I had not heard from him. At that time, he had asked if he could come down and visit us. We had adamantly told him that it was a very bad time to visit. We emphatically told him that it would not be a good time, because Allissa had just had a baby, our third child delivered by C-section, and needed to recover from the operation. After a brief greeting on this particular call, Joe said, "I am in Richmond right now and will need a ride once I get to the Greenville, SC bus station. I decided that I wanted to come down and spend some time with you. See you then." After the initial shock I said to my wife, "Allissa, guess who is coming for Christmas?" She asked, "Who?" I said, "My old friend, Slow Joe." She asked, "Where would he stay and for how long?" I told her that I did not have an answer to either of those questions.

All I knew was two things: where and when to pick him up at the bus station and that there was no way we would have him stay with us. One may ask, "Why would you not want Slow Joe living with you?" That is a long story. Joe had been divorced and had been living with various women until they got wise to his games and gave him the boot. Joe also had been struggling with alcohol and drug addictions, gambling and theft-related problems. Due to his lifestyle, he was a hunted man from both sides of the law. Joe also had survived several life-threatening accidents, but they had taken their toll on his body in the form of pins and stitches. He almost lost his left arm as he left it dangling out the window of his car as he drove drunk down the PA turnpike and hit the concrete median between the two lanes, sandwiching his left arm.

Now Joe wanted to live with us in sunny South Carolina. At this time I had been the pastor of University Baptist Church for five years. We also had many friends in piney South Carolina. I immediately called my friend, and chairman of the deacon board, Marshall A. Fant, III.

I explained to Brother Marsh that we did not feel comfortable having Joe stay with us. We also truly did not have any room in our 1140 square-foot house for a house-guest. We had just put in a contract on a 3,000 square-foot house with Mrs. Granberg which would give us more room to minister. This was one time we were glad that we did not have more room to minister. Also, Allissa was not fully recovered from her surgery and did not need any additional pressures at that time. In fact, we had already decided that we would stay in Clemson for Christmas, rather than make the trek to see our families in Pennsylvania. We had determined that this year we would celebrate a nice, quiet, restful, Christmas at home. At this time the church was renting the little house next to the church for Sunday school space, called the Welborn House. I asked Marsh if we could put Slow Joe there if I put together some house rules that he would have to maintain. The house rules were similar to the guidelines at Alcatraz. At the first infraction it was stated he would have to go.

With the housing problem temporarily solved, I went to pick up my long-time friend of some twenty years. At the bus station Joe gave me a big hug. We then lugged his 20 inch TV, his weights and his clothes to the pastor mobile, an 85 Buick LeSabre. What I placed in the boot was all of Joe's earthly possessions. It was strange to be with Slow Joe in South Carolina. The last and only time we were in South Carolina together was in January of 1975, some fourteen years earlier when we had run away from home.

My how things had changed! Joe and I got a hoagie at Subway. It was no southern Philly or Bill Morris Hoagie, but it still hit the spot. My wife and boys greeted Joe warmly once we got home. We had prepped them and our church folks of the need of seeing Slow Joe get saved. Many were praying and anxious to meet the one that they had heard about in many a sermon illustration. For most, the Christmas Eve service would be their first introduction to this friend of infamy. The first to meet Joe were the Fants as they came early to church to prepare for the Christmas Eve service. Joe looked like a choir boy as he helped straighten the hymn books on the metal chairs when the Fants came in. Many introductions were made. Joe was on his best behavior that night.

Everything was very new for Joe with his old friend Will. The last time Joe and I were together we were drinking beer and smoking with Mary Jane. Now his former pagan buddy was reading the Christmas story and talking about the love of God and the free gift of salvation. Now he had new friends that called him Pastor.

It was all somewhat amusing to him. It was like the old Will was dead and that there was a resurrected new Will. Slow Joe would test the new Will to see if the old Will was still around. I told him that he was not, that he died in October of 1979 in a terrible battle.

The next day was Christmas. What an unusual Christmas day it would be. Our family was enjoying one of God's most recent gifts to our family: baby Benjamin. John and Jim were excited about their Christmas gifts: a bicycle and a big wheel. Slow Joe was also enjoying the toys we got him. Apparently they were not enough, because the boys caught him stealing their candy. I told the boys to forgive and to pray for Joe. I also related to them how as a young boy Joe would come to our house and steal the candy out of the candy jar. It became quite a habit, so our family began to put all our stale candies and cookies, dog biscuits, etc. in the jar just for Joe. We would then howl after Joe would go home when we would take stock of what was missing from the candy jar. That evening we celebrated Christmas at the house of Jo Ann Mattress. She had cooked an incredible feast. The last time Joe and I were in South Carolina Joe was stealing moon pies from a black woman. Now we were both enjoying sweet potato pies from the heart and hands of one of our dearest black friends.

Between Christmas and New Year's Day, Slow Joe went jogging with the group, which would later be known as the Sea Turtles. Watching Joe run made me hurt for him. He now ran like the Tin Man in the Wizard of Oz. He could still shake and bake, but the grace and speed that he once had was gone. Joe, in high school, had set records in the 220 and 440-yard runs. He had received a full track scholarship in Florida and was not too far from competing with some of the big boys that you see race every four years. Growing up, I always thought I was really slow when Joe and I would work out together. Now for the first time, I beat Joe and had to wait for him as we jogged 4 miles around the dikes of Clemson.

Joe was able to find some work with a landscaper, who was very kind to pick him up each day. Joe had earlier lost his driver's license as a result of his drinking and drug addictions. We were still praying and hoping that Joe would get saved. He attended the services as required for staying in the Welborn House.

One night Joe came in late to the prayer meeting and overheard Lulu Simpleton (a very sporadic visitor) ask prayer for her estranged husband. Lulu did not see Joe enter the service and sit in the back row. After prayer meeting, Joe and I went to BiLo to pick up some milk and food for the next day. Joe happened to wander off in the store, which always left me feeling uncomfortable. I would have preferred him staying next to me to eat his animal cookies, but he had a mind of his own. As he wandered down the aisles he ran into Lulu shopping. He sneaked up to her and said, "Hello Lulu, I am praying for you and your husband Elvis." Joe had the luxury of seeing and hearing Lulu at church, but Lulu had never met, heard of, or seen Joe. She stood in amazement that this perfect stranger would know her name and her husband's name and that she was having marital problems. She then in a whisper asked Joe, "Are you an angel?"

Joe was no angel. Joe began to slip out at night to respond to the call of the Wild. One good thing was that he did witness for our church in places where we had never ventured before. Despite our hell's angel, the Lord used Joe at Tiger Town Tavern. He met one girl who had a Christian roommate, who was looking not for a bar, but for a church. After meeting "this neat guy" at the pub, she went back to her apartment to inform her roommate of the good church she had heard of from this angel. Her roommate did come and visit the church and stayed at UBC till her graduation. Some of her friends also came and several made decisions for the Lord. Joe was becoming quite an evangelist for UBC.

I discussed with our men that Joe had violated our house rules and that I would have to ask him to leave. They also agreed that it probably wasn't the best for Joe to be our ambassador at each of the local taverns, where he advertised our church and the great fellowship that he was having with the pastor as he stayed at the church's prophet chamber.

It was Saturday, January 13, 1990, when I confronted Joe and said that he would have to leave. He had no money and no transportation. I told him that he needed to choose a place he wanted to go, and that on Monday I would take him there. That night Joe got wasted and got into a fight at one of the bars. For once he looked like he was on the short end of the stick. He came straggling into church late the next morning. Anyone standing within 15 feet of Slow Joe was in danger of getting a buzz. Joe stayed for the pot-luck dinner that we had scheduled at church that day.

I knew that he would begin to sober up maybe before the evening service and that this would be the last service I would have officially to preach to him. I set aside my regular message and that afternoon loaded my 22, 12-gauge, 30-06, bazooka and patriot missiles with every verse in the Bible that dealt with drunkenness. The sacred text I settled on was I Timothy 1:14, and the message title was, "The Greatest Sinner That Ever Lived." I went on to preach about every converted drunk I knew of from John Newton to Billy Sunday, to Will Senn. I preached against bars, harlots, wormy Tequila, Jack Daniels, Budweiser and the Bloody Mary. My three points were: The Sinner, The Savior and The Saint. I then gave the invitation to my audience of one while everybody else prayed. Slow Joe stood up and that night came forward at the invitation.

I had already determined if he responded to the message that Mr. Kent Edwards would be my choice to counsel him. Mr. Edwards took Slow Joe back into the counseling room and literally wept for his soul to be saved. Slow Joe had never seen anyone weep for his soul before and this melted him as he bent on his knees to ask Jesus Christ to save his soul. We don't always know what transpires in the human heart. Time is generally the best test to see if someone meant business for the Lord or not. If one is truly repentant they will not want to return to the sin that nailed Christ to the cross. True saving faith, is the faith that changes the life. That night we had the hope that maybe Slow Joe got saved. That night for the first time we had Slow Joe spend the night with us on the living room couch.

The next day marked the day that I would literally take Joe anywhere outside of South Carolina. I asked Joe if he wanted to go back to Pennsylvania or New Jersey or Delaware. Joe's choice was Florida. He wanted to go to sunny Daytona Beach. I said, "Fine, let's go." Joe and I then got into our van to start the journey. I also took Jimbo who was 2 ½ years old. Our first stop on the trip was the pawnshop in Clemson. As Joe pawned his TV set it struck me that the last and only time I had been in a pawnshop was with you-know-who on the second Monday of January 1975.

It then began to hit me what the Lord was doing for me. This trip and time with Joe would parallel as well as contrast our first trip to Florida together. It was now the second Monday of January 1990, the exact day of the same month when we set off for Florida fourteen years earlier. After Joe had his $100 in hand we took off to Florida. We then took a route that would have nearly paralleled our first trip. As we traveled through Georgia, I was craving a moon pie. I looked at Joe who was sleeping and began to fight back tears. I said, "Lord there go I, apart from the grace of God." Joe still smelled like booze and was wearing soiled pants, his hair was greasy. The message was clear, apart from God's redeeming love; I would still have been on the same path of self-destruction or even dead. God wanted to impress upon my heart His "Amazing Grace."

In the back seat, Jim was asleep. How different! I had a wife, a family, and a church that loved me. Joe was divorced, had a son he was not permitted to see and had no church home. I had peace, joy and purpose for living. Joe had confusion, a hangover, and no direction for life. The difference in the comparison was God. I had salvation, the indwelling Spirit of God and the Scriptures. Joe had been a child of the devil, was dominated by his fleshly desires and had been conformed to the world. I prayed for Joe as he slept. I was able to hide my emotions when Joe awoke. I was looking for a Kentucky Fried Chicken, but could not find one. We settled for McDonalds.

After a full-day's drive, we arrived finally in Daytona Beach. That Monday night, just like that Monday night fourteen years earlier, we stayed in a motel together. He slept with his head set on listening to music. I slept with Jim, listening to him. In the middle of the night Joe woke me up and asked for my keys to get something out of the van. It was now decision time. Do I give him the keys or say, "No, I'll get what you need." I knew there was a good likelihood that he would take off with my van, never to be seen again. Memories of him leaving me at a gas station in New Jersey to hitch hike home to PA flooded my mind. It was at that point that I gave Joe the keys in a symbolic gesture of trust and friendship. I prayed, and he actually returned to the room.

Before leaving Joe the next day, I had two objectives: to find him a fundamental, Bible-believing church and a place to live. After looking at the Yellow Pages, the decision of a church was made very easy. There was a fundamental, Baptist church near by with a pastor whose name was Daniel Webster. With my love for history and my own peculiar name as a pastor, I knew this had to be the church. After meeting with Pastor Webster, objective number one was met. He would do his best to help Joe. I told him what a blessing he would be to the church's outreach program and how he was very good at pioneering new areas of ministry.

The second objective, being Joe's need of housing, was met through the pastor's recommendation to inquire at a particular housing complex. There I talked with the Hungarian manager and explained my mission. He was willing to work with Slow Joe. I then paid him for the rent and helped move Joe into his new one-room house. There was not much to move in, but there was much to move out. Joe and I then hugged each other. I told him I loved him and that I would be praying for him. Then I said good-bye to Slow Joe and took off for home sweet home with Jim.

As we drove away, I could not keep the tears back any longer and the ducts began to pour out a mixture of relief and sorrow. Jim asked, "Why are you crying Daddy?" I simply said, "Let's go home." There is no place like home. There is no place like home. There is no place like home.

SIX YEARS LATER

It was a Friday night, February 7, 1996, and we had just finished dinner when the phone rang. Usually the phone rings during dinner so we knew it was someone we probably didn't know. I had been sick so my wife answered the phone and talked for a moment and then she said, "Guess who is on the phone." I had no idea. (Would you like to make a guess?) As I picked up the phone, I said, "Hello." On the other end was a pleasant voice, with a southern accent. The person introduced herself as Mrs. Iniz Rollins. She said, "Do you remember who I am?" After a brief pause, I said, "Yes, I remember a Mrs. Rollins who helped me some twenty-one years ago when I ran away from home with Slow Joe." She went on to explain that the strangest thing had happened that day. While she was cleaning out her desk she found two old letters which had slipped under the drawers. The first letter was written with the following letterhead, 'William J. Senn,' followed by a short letter written with a red flair pen.

There was a second letter joined to the first letter, which had the following letterhead 'Mrs. William J. Senn, Jr.' followed by a short letter written with a blue flair pen. The two letters read:

                                        William J. Senn
                                        Dowlin Forge Road
                                        Downingtown, Pa.
                                        269-4311

Dear Mrs. Rollins,

I cannot thank you enough in loaning me the twenty dollars.
It was just enough to get me and my so-called friend to North
Carolina where our parents had telegrammed us some money. We
then arrived home at 4:00 a.m. in the morning where we were
met by our loving parents, upset but glad to see us. The
snow had made slow driving but with your help and a little
from above we made it. I thank-you so very much.

Lov ya!
Will Senn
P.S. Glad to see there is still a little trust in the world!

(On the back of the letter I wrote 24 — "Thank You's!")

```
                          Mrs. William J. Senn, Jr.
                          Dowlin Forge Road, R.D. #2
                          Downing Town, PENNA.  19335
February 7, 1975
Dear Mrs. Rollins,
```

We are ever so grateful for not only the loan of money to our son, but, the trust you gave him. Thank you so very much.

I do hope they learned something from their trip — I know he did from you — I thank you for that also.

His father and I were a wreck from worry, but we all seem to have bounced back. I hope there are no repeat performances.

```
Thank you again ever so much.
Sincerely yours,
Allison C. Senn
```

(At the bottom of the letter was my name later added by Mrs. Rollins, my phone number and address in Clemson.)

The voice on the other end of the phone said, "When I found the letters, I noticed that the date of the letters were February 7, 1975. I could not believe it, because today is February 7, 1996. Exactly twenty-one years later. I was so impressed with this "coincidence" that I thought I would write you a letter to your old address, but then I noticed your phone number on the letterhead and determined to call and see if by any chance I could reach you. I called, but the phone was disconnected. I then called information to see if there were any Senns still living in that area code. The operator gave me the number of a William J. Senn, Jr. in Coatesville, so I called that number. A woman by the name of Lynn answered the phone and readily gave me your phone number and address in South Carolina. So I decided to call you and see how you were doing."

I was absolutely stunned that she would go to such measures to reach a perfect stranger who she had met only once some twenty-one years before. I then began to tell her that I was now married and had three wonderful boys. I also told her I was a pastor, hoping that this would open up a door to witness to this dear lady who

106

helped me in my time of need. As soon as I told Mrs. Rollins that I was a born-again Christian and a pastor of a Baptist Church, I knew that I had hit a chord. There was a brief pause in the conversation as I waited to hear her first impressions of her prodigal friend come home. She then went on to tell me that after she and her husband had helped Joe and I with the loan of $20.00 that she prayed for me. Her prayers did not stop there, for she told her friends in her Bible-believing, Baptist church to pray for two young men who needed the Lord by the name of Will and Joe. She said she had lost my letter and consequently had forgotten our last names, but for twenty-one years she had prayed off and on for a boy by the name of "Will" to be saved. Now on the phone, tears of joy were being shed, for God had abundantly answered her prayer. *"Now unto him that is able to do exceedingly abundantly above all that we ask or think, according to the power that worketh in us"* (Ephesians 3:20). Not only had I become a Christian by asking the Lord Jesus to forgive me of my sins and to enter my heart to be my Savior and Lord, but I was in the Lord's work as a pastor. She said she couldn't wait to tell her friends at church on Sunday about God's answer to prayer. I said the same! We talked for a few more minutes and I told her about Slow Joe and how I had not heard from him in six years. I told her to keep praying for him, then we said our good-byes.

After hanging up I stood in shock and began to well up with tears. Here was a woman who had prayed for my soul twenty-one years earlier having no idea if her prayers had yet been answered or not. Then the Lord rewarded her faithfulness by pulling out of hiding two letters written exactly twenty-one years prior to her discovery. God's timing was perfect. Several days later I received a letter from Mrs. Rollins with two letters enclosed.

Her letter is as follows:

February 7, 1996
21 years later

Will and family,

I was so happy to hear your voice Friday night. I have prayed and wondered about you and the other boy for so long. I prayed for "Will," so can I still call you that? Thank God you got home safe, so many kids don't. I have two children and two grandchildren and I pray if they ever need help away from home a Christian person will send them home.

I know your parents are proud of you and what you have become. I know God is the answer to all our problems, believe me without Him I couldn't have gone through what I have with my daughter. She has asthma and we know prayers are answered. I just hope your friend will turn around and trust the Lord.

I sure enjoyed your church letter that is so interesting the way you keep notes daily. Yes, I hope we can keep in touch because we have another friend in Christ. Maybe our paths will cross in person one day, who knows.

Thanks so much,
In Christian love,
Iniz Rollins

P.S. I thought you and your family would enjoy your own letter. Thanks.

Along with her letter, Mrs. Rollins sent me a check for $20.00. This was the amount that I had borrowed from her and her husband twenty-one years earlier. Allissa and I both smiled. I instantly told Allissa what we needed to do with this $20.00. We would set it aside and give it to the next run-away that came our way in the ministry. We then prayed that God would send us a run-away that we could tell our story of God's redeeming grace. Remarkably the next day we had a knock on our door. It was a young man we had ministered to by the nickname, Peanut. He had a distressed, young lady with him that he had picked up on I-85 hitchhiking. He told us that he did not know what to do with her but thought of us and that maybe we could help her. He then dropped her off with us. While Allissa made her dinner I listened to her story. She made me feel a little uncomfortable and I determined that it would be better for her to stay at the Tiger Town Motel with our Indian friends rather than at the Senn Bed and Breakfast. After dinner and her need to smoke a cigarette we took our guest to the motel and checked her in. Before leaving her and assuring her that we would pick her up for church in the morning. I told her my story of how I had run away and how a Christian woman by the name of Iniz Rollins had helped me and prayed for me. I told our runaway that we would likewise pray for her. I presented her with God's wonderful plan of salvation. She did not want to accept the Lord as her Savior at this time. I respected her refusal, but my spirit was heavy, knowing that her greatest need was salvation. I then presented her with a $20 bill and explained how we had just prayed the day before that God would send us someone on the run. I gave it to her and shared that it was my prayer that someday she would become a Christian and that she would have the opportunity to help a runaway with a similar gift of $20.00. I then prayed for her and went home. The next morning Allissa and I returned to the motel to pick up our friend but she was gone. The worker at the desk said she left right after we dropped her off and that they wouldn't charge for the room since she did not stay. I am not sure where she went, but the Lord does. Perhaps twenty-one years later we will hear that she became a Christian and has a ministry with those who are running from God. Why not?

THREE YEARS LATER

Three years later, DECEMBER 22, 1999 we are now near to celebrating the last Christmas of this millennium. My wife, Allissa, my children (John – 14, Jim –12, and Benjamin 10) and myself would like to wish you all a Merry Christmas and a Happy New Year.

It is our prayer that each of our family members and friends will have a Christ-filled Holiday Season. God answers prayers. I am so glad that someone cared for my soul and prayed that I would become a Christian. Eternity will only tell how many of our prayers have been answered as it concerns our praying for those who do not have a personal relationship with Christ.

To have such a personal relationship, one must acknowledge that they are a sinner. Our conscience does a good job of condemning us when we do wrong. It brings to our mind the verdict that we are guilty before a holy God. Sadly, many ignore the work of the conscience or run from its convicting work. Even more tragic, is for people to seek religion rather than a relationship with Christ to somehow atone for their own sins. Jesus said, *"Not every one that saith unto me, Lord, Lord, shall enter into the kingdom of heaven; but he that doeth the will of my Father which is in heaven. Many will say to me in that day, Lord, Lord, have we not prophesied in thy name? And in thy name have cast out devils? And in thy name done many wonderful works? And then will I profess unto them, I never knew you: depart from me ye that work iniquity* (Matthew 7:21-23)."

There will sadly be many who in the Day of Judgment, who will find that their name was not written in the Lamb's book of life! Just like twenty-five years ago, I thought that I would find my name on the team's roster. How surprised I was not to find my name on the list. I had played many basketball games, I had scored a lot of points, I had practiced for hours shooting foul shots, I had worked hard to get in shape, yet my efforts were not enough. Tragically, *"many"* will say they had taught Sunday school, given to charity, were a member of a church, been christened or baptized, but will be surprised to find that they were not truly on God's team. The reason being is that they had trusted their own good works rather than the finished work of Christ on the cross. God explicitly states that our religious efforts will never save us. Ephesians 2:8-9 spells out that salvation is a gift that no one can earn. *"For by grace are ye saved through faith; and that not of yourselves: it is the gift of God: Not of works, lest any man should boast."*

There will be a day when the Lord will open the book of life to reveal the names of those who have been saved by faith. *"Many"* will be surprised not to find their name on God's roster. Revelation 20:15 reads, *"And whosover was not found written in the book of life was cast into the lake of fire."* A true child of God is one who entered into a personal relationship with God through faith alone.

Well I have got to run, someone is on the phone and my wife just cried out, "Will, Guess who is coming for Christmas?" I wonder who that could be? Apparently, the last chapter for this story has not been written!

CHAPTER ELEVEN

I SURVIVED THE CHATTOOGA RIVER OR I SURVIVED UNIVERSITY BAPTIST CHURCH'S MISSION CONFERENCE

I t was Saturday, October 10, 1998, the opening day of our annual mission's conference. The conference was to begin with the Sea Turtle "fun run." The Sea Turtle race is 3.1 miles (5K) in distance and is a real challenge to see which missionaries and pastors are in shape. The usual response when the missionaries see the event in their informational packet is, "Are you kidding, do we really have to run 3.1 miles?" This year we had sixty runners participating. The person who comes in first receives the Sea Hawk award and the person who comes in last receives the Sea Slug award. The most coveted award is the Sea Turtle award given to the runner who finishes the race with the closest time to 25:00 minutes without going under it.

Many factors are involved in the Sea Turtle formula. The runner first guesses his actual time to complete the race (He cannot run wearing a watch). The difference between his guestimate and the actual time is added to the actual time. Then the formula gets sticky, for the runner is then to subtract one second from his actual time for each year of his life. He then is permitted to take off one second from his actual time for each pound that he weighs. When all the numbers are placed in the formula and computed I strangely have a time right around 25:00. This year my fudged finish was 25:04. As fate would have it however, little nine-year old Brian

Horton finished with a computed time of 25:01. All I could think of was that I would certainly win next year's race.

Don Clipperton won the award for the fastest missionary from Argentina. He was the only runner from Argentina. Dave Utter won the award for the fastest runner from the Marshall Islands. He was the only runner from the Marshall Islands. John Anderson won the award for the fastest 5K from a missionary from China and aged Bill Kieffer won the award for being the fastest runner from Brazil. I think Bill Kieffer also won the Sea Slug award. Very unusual to win the race in your category and still come in last, go figure!

After the race, I quickly raced to the airport to pick up sixty-seven year old Bill Heffley from Pennsylvania. Bill had been warned by Mel Skiles to stay away from Will Senn, and after Bill's last trip to South Carolina, such warning was well justified. On Bill's first trip to South Carolina, he was almost killed on a mountain bike trip around Issaqueena Lake when he hit a tree head on and rolled down the embankment almost into his watery grave. Bill never saw the tree and was pretty banged up from the hit. His shirt was ruined and his pride affected. Barry Milsaps warned Bill as well to stay away from Will Senn, because strange things happen around the man.

Bill is a retired chemist who fought his industry as a whistle blower. He was fired for his outcries against beryllium as his company polluted the Surekill River with their chemicals. Bill is a real naturalist, fisherman, outdoorsman and baseball fanatic and coach. We were thrilled to have Bill for the mission's conference and hoped that he would enjoy his time with the missionaries. We wanted Bill to have a memorable time and selfishly we were hoping that he would consider moving down to South Carolina to join our ministry and family.

Saturday afternoon we took the missionaries to the Clemson – Maryland football game. It was a beautiful day to hear Tiger Rag and to watch the Tigers mop up the Terrapins. On Sunday, the conference was building with excitement as we heard the missionaries preach and present their burden for preaching the gospel. We had a wonderful Lord's Day with our guests. I also met with the missionaries to explain to them the week of events and to go over our plans for Monday. The year before was a big hit, with my wife Allissa taking the missionary wives to Commerce, Georgia, to go shopping at the outlet malls with money that the church gave them.

The men the year before had joined me for a casual canoe trip down Section II of the Chattooga River. All I remember of that Saturday trip was two of our missionaries capsizing their canoe at Big Shoals, and hearing the moans of Eric Fisher for 7 miles on the river. All he wanted to do was read a book and/or watch the Penn State football game against Illinois. Eric would have preferred going to a bookstore over a canoe ride down the Chattooga. How hopelessly boring! The only redeeming feature about the canoe ride with Eric was the enthusiasm his wife shared for the trip and the occasional scream when we splashed him with water with our paddles. All in our party thought that he would melt.

This year I was toying with taking the men to the same river but this time down Section III that I had not previously attempted. To prepare for this year's adventure, I had purchased a book called *The Chattooga Wild and Scenic River* by Brian Boyd, which I actually read and had placed with my other books at church.

Sunday night Allissa and I reviewed the highlights of the day and began to discuss the logistics for the next day's events. I told her I was going to take the men down Section III. When she heard that she strongly sought to persuade me to reconsider. Allissa wanted me to take the men down Section II. Allissa and I had been down that section several times and had enjoyed it very much. On our first trip we used our canoe and attempted to tow our three boys behind us on inner tubes. I have to admit this was somewhat of a disaster, and I can still see Ben's horrified face when he saw his mother fall out of the canoe backwards and disappear under the white water rapids. Also, on that maiden voyage we ran across one of our families at church fishing on the banks. Was Mrs. Anita Nicholson ever surprised when she saw her pastor navigating his canoe with John, Jim, Ben and Allissa floating by at her fishing hole at the bend of the river!

Allissa and I debated the wisdom of going down Section III for over an hour. Finally, after midnight, we ran the white flag up the pole and tried to get some sleep before the big day. Regardless of what section we chose to run, I told her that I would take good care of our missionaries and that I would be home in time to help John with his bug project which was due Tuesday. Not only was she afraid for the physical safety of the group, she was concerned that we did not have enough time to complete the trip in time for the 7:00 p.m. evening service. She reminded me that the missionaries needed to get back in time to get cleaned up and changed, have dinner with their host families in the church and be adequately prepared for the service. I reassured her that I would be back by 3:00 p.m. Allissa pleaded with me with great "anguish of spirit" to listen.

The morning of Monday, October 12, 1998 arrived. For my devotions that morning I read Exodus 6:9, *"And Moses spake so unto the children of Israel: but they hearkened not unto Moses for anguish of spirit."* My own journal notes regarding the text said, "no one listens." When the preacher does not listen you know the people will be in trouble and in bondage and will not be able to "cross over" the Red Sea or the Chattooga. The word Chattooga or Chatuga is a Cherokee word which means, "we crossed here." The Cherokees may have borrowed the word from the Creek Indians, which makes better sense for Creeks to name rivers.

I side-stepped Allissa's question as to what section we would be going on, and encouraged her to get a move on to church to meet the wives for the big shopping trip. I hurried down to the church to find my book on the Chattooga in my library. Once in my office I looked everywhere for my book. I wanted to read to the group the various points on the river where the most folks had drowned. I also wanted to review what the book said regarding how to negotiate such sections.

Since 1970, there has been an average of 1.2 deaths on the Chattooga. The most dangerous spots are the Bull Sluice with nine deaths, Woodall Shoals with seven deaths, the Five Falls area with eleven deaths, the Narrows with three deaths, etc. Eleven of the last thirty-five deaths on the river were a result of inappropriate floating devices. Typically, those who die on the river, die as a result of head wounds, exposure, foot entrapment, caught in the current or hydraulics, hypothermia, pinned in the river, caught under a tree that has fallen, etc. As I wrote this story (November 2003) I received word that another expert kayaker was killed on the river after doing a "wet exit" out of his kayak and getting trapped in the Crack-in-the-Rock rapid. The force of the water at this rapid at 10 feet under is rated at 10,000 pounds per square inch. It took rescuers one week to get his body out of the rapid.

The good news is that there has never been a fatality on the river involving a commercial trip that includes a river tour guide. Allissa asked if we could get a guide from one of the rafting companies. I told her that this would not be necessary since I had read the book and was going to take along Art Johns' waterproof map. My biggest fears were navigating the Narrows and the infamous Bull Sluice. The map would alert us to these dangers in advance and we would be able to line up the best routes.

I could not find the book, so I settled for a book on miracles to motivate the crew on the journey ahead. We kissed our wives good bye and hopped in my River Rod station wagon and Chuck Horton's minivan. On the way to the river we traveled through Seneca and then Walhalla. We stopped at Subway to pick up subs for lunch but found Subway was not open yet. Consequently, we stopped at Ingles and picked up the necessary drinks and food for a great picnic on the river. Most importantly, we stocked up on Oreo cookies and Fig Newtons. I was starving and probably should have had breakfast, but the prospects of a big lunch on the banks of the Chattooga gave me good incentive to be patient, and to chow later.

On the way up Highway 28 we stopped at the Ranger's House next to Stumphouse Tunnel. Art Johns, our fearless leader, wanted to get information on the water level of the river. This is important information to gauge how long it will take to float a section, as well as to see the severity of the flow of the river. The Chattooga is extremely steep, dropping an average of 49 feet per mile, which exceeds the pace of the famed Colorado River (A river the author can't wait to go down with the missionaries at Tri-City Baptist Church during our next mission's conference). The river in its entirety is 57 miles in length. We were only going to do the 13 miles of Section III. I knew the water level was going to be low, but you can never be too safe.

Near to the Ranger's House are the remains of the Blue Ridge railroad project and the 4,000 feet Stumphouse Tunnel. The project came to a screeching halt in 1861. The reason was the accursed "Yankees." The project was to connect Charleston with Cincinnati, Ohio. Sherman was from Ohio. In 1861 no Rebel in his right mind wanted to go to Ohio, nor did they want Yankees to come south. Now on top of the Tunnel stood a new Sherman who was ready to take the Chattooga on by storm.

There was no ranger in sight so we proceeded to Earl's Ford where we dropped off the boats, the drinks, the food, and the apprehensive missionaries. On the road I did all I could to magnify what the U.S. Congress meant by designating the Chattooga a "Wild, scenic and recreational" river. "Wild" means that there are 40 miles of river that rev up adrenaline of real men. "Scenic" means that there are 2 miles of river that has undeveloped shoreline that is accessible by road and is enjoyed by real women from their cars. For real men this translates into a canoe trip that is surrounded by 15,000 acres of land that is not accessible by road. Which translates into either a helicopter rescue, an exit by death, or you complete the section on the water. "Recreational" means that lake kayaks can be used to navigate the class one and two rapids.

After dropping off the gang, Chuck and I took the two vehicles to the parking lot at the end of Section III. It took us about thirty minutes to get there. After leaving my station wagon for the return trip, hiding my keys and wallet, paying the parking fee, Chuck Horton drove us back in his van in about fifteen minutes. On several occasions I asked Chuck how his spiritual life was as we leaned through the turns. Chuck said that he and Joan were going to join our church. Chuck also offered me an apple, which I readily devoured. My stomach was growling. Once re-united with our party at Earl's Ford we took a picture of the team. We then all looked at the river. I felt like Hernando De Soto who had marched his small army by this river in 1540 in search of gold. We were looking for a different gold. The gold that comes from completing a successful challenge!

I looked up the river to familiar territory, Section II, 7 miles of flat and calm water. Section II has a gradient of 12 feet per mile, with a width of 25-100 feet. Acceptable levels for floating this section are from .8 to 3.5 feet. We had floated the whole range of waters a half dozen times on Section II. The worst part of this section is Big Shoals, a class three rapid, and the ¼ mile uphill hike to haul the canoes to the River Rod.

Now I looked down stream. I had no idea what was ahead of us for the next 13 miles, and neither did anyone else. I did know that there lurked a handful of class four rapids and the Bull Sluice, a class five. There are six classes of rapids with class one and two rapids being the easiest, class three being medium in difficulty, class four is difficult, class five is very difficult and class six extraordinarily difficult. While I looked up and down the river, Chuck Horton gave a mini-clinic to the neophytes on how to paddle. His class began with the following instructions, "This is a paddle."

I first got into Art John's green kayak, the Keowee. The Keowee has a hull designed for lakes and not for whitewater. I don't believe I had ever been in a kayak. I placed the waterproof map on the dash or whatever you call the front of a kayak. Behind me in my 17 foot Coleman lake canoe were Don Clipperton and John Anderson and all of our food and drinks in a Coleman picnic container, followed by Bill Heffley, Chuck Horton and Art Johns. Bill would sit in the middle and get a free ride from the neurological nurse and from the Grassman. The Chattooga is not very user friendly for canoes with three members. Dave Utter and Bill Kieffer were in Pat Buckley's 15 foot Coleman lake canoe. The team numbered eight and all had registered their name on the information board. There was no one else on the register. We had the river all to ourselves!

Leading the way we went around the first bend. There in the middle of the water were two deer. What a phenomenal sight, immediately Psalm 42:1 came to my mind, "As the hart [deer] panteth after the water brooks, so panteth my soul after thee, O God." They scurried down stream a bit and then up into the woods. Then right in front of us we encountered "War-woman Rapid." I thought to myself, who named these rapids? Did some Indian have a fight with his woman before going down these rapids? Was he scalped? We all had trouble negotiating this class three rapid. We did not dump our boats, but it sure wasn't pretty. On the banks of the river was a sign that had words to the effect, "If you had trouble negotiating this rapid please turn back."

Just a few hundred yards down the river I lost control of my kayak in what at best would be classified a class two rapid. It was very embarrassing to have everyone chase after my oar as I tried to get myself back in the craft. This was not a good sign. One mile down the river we encountered the Rock Garden. We did not see one flower in the midst but did see massive granite slabs embedded in the river. The rocks looked like fingers waving good bye. Up to this point I was the only one to have capsized. However, that would change quickly at Dick's Creek Ledge. Off to the side was a spectacular 50 foot waterfall. In front of us was thundering whitewater and the need of a strong S-maneuver over a double drop. Dick's Creek lived up to its class four rating. The only near casualty was the Chuck Horton and Bill Kieffer canoe, which was taking in much water and was sinking. They had to get out of the canoe and empty the craft of hundreds of gallons of water. Bill Heffley had a smirk on his face and made some clever comments about the Titanic sinking.

I impressed myself with my S-maneuver which I proudly thought stood for Senn-maneuver. However, "pride cometh before a fall" in this case a small waterfall and the Stair-steps, a class three rapid, chewed me up. I found myself pinned against a "step" in about 2 feet of water. I was facing upstream and could not move at first. I thought how stupid to die in 2 feet of water. How do you explain that feat? Finally, I was able to shift my weight around and spin out. Again I lost my oar, and again someone had to fetch it. Somehow during all this I was able to keep my map from floating away.

I knew we had gone about 3 miles into the trip and that the Narrows was immanent. I wanted to get in front of everyone and stop and get out before we went through the Narrows, a very complex class four rapid that extends 150 yards. While I tried to paddle and orient myself to the river and the map, I concluded that we were approaching the upper half of a long series of ledges that were funneling down in width. It looked like the river was narrowing rapidly. Perhaps this was the Narrows.

As I slowed to look at my map, John Anderson and Don Clipperton went paddling by picking up speed. I screamed, "I think this is the Narrows, stay on the Georgia side of the river." I watched in horror as they navigated through some big waves and picked up speed as they entered the Narrows, a 10 foot wide slot between two massive rock formations. Somehow they got their canoe turned around. Despite going backwards through the Narrows it looked like they were going to make it safely to the emerald pool ahead; and then out of nowhere they flipped over. It looked like they were having trouble so I paddled ahead to help pick up the pieces.

I was a little nervous going through the shoot and I paddled ferociously to take the line closest to the Georgia side, which I recalled reading in my lost book was the safest line. The current was so strong that it pulled me to the South Carolina side where I knew I was going to be bashed on the jutting formation on the left. As I braced myself for the hit, my kayak capsized. I felt the cutback current pulling on me in a massive undertow force. Somehow I was thrown from the kayak and landed in the mid-stream of the Narrows and near to my kayak, which I grabbed with all of the strength that I had and floated out of danger.

Unfortunately, my map floated off on the top of the water. I was able to keep pace with my map but could never catch up. I watched it sink right in front of me. I thought of diving under to get it but was somewhat fearful of the underwater currents. All the rocks in this section are extremely undercut and therefore very dangerous. As John and Don pulled me up, we watched one floating device and an oar go merrily, merrily down the stream and now life was not a dream. Also, I noticed that all of our food and all of our drinks had been lost from John's canoe at the Narrows. We now had 10 miles left in our adventure and no food or drink for the remainder of the day. I thought how glad I was that I had eaten that apple.

Don was pretty shook up. Looking at his pants I could understand. They were shredded down one side. John was doing fine, but he was noticeably troubled with the loss of food. The main reason was that he was a diabetic. Fortunately, Chuck somehow had salvaged a peanut butter sandwich which John would woof down.

As we looked back upstream we saw Chuck, Bill Heffley and Art try to negotiate the Narrows. Again the current pulled them to the South Carolina side and rolled their canoe. Chuck held onto the canoe but the undertow was so strong that it pulled off his boat shoes. We were not able to reach their oars and floating device as it went down stream. Art nonchalantly swam out of danger as if it was old-hat.

Bill, the senior citizen on the trip, had shared earlier with me his fear of water that resulted from a near-drowning childhood experience. I knew if Bill survived the Narrows, he would be cured for life. I watched Bill hold onto his canoe for dear life. He survived! It was the first time that I was ever with Bill that he could not talk. He was white as a ghost.

Just at this time we saw two angels of light coming down the river in two kayaks. These boaters would be the only people we would see on the river all day. The woman went first and had the same problem we had, but was able to do an Eskimo Roll and pull out of the Narrows. The man was able to negotiate the currents flawlessly. Their timing was perfect; they saw our plight of losing our oars down stream and made a beeline after them. They were able to find all the oars but one and placed them on the shoreline as they continued on their merry way.

Just after they passed by, Dave Utter and Bill Kieffer began their trek down the Narrows. We watched what looked to be a slow motion replay of John and Don, and Art, Bill and Chuck as Dave and Bill's canoe capsized. Bill Kieffer was being pulled under but was able to roll out of the undertow. Bill later shared that growing up in California he had learned to roll out of the undertows in the ocean rather than fight them. Bill and Dave were both able to float out of danger, but oddly their canoe had disappeared. We waited for their canoe to float by under water or to surface, but it never did. We pulled everyone up to the rock I was standing on to regroup. Fortunately, there were still eight in the party, but we were now missing one canoe. That would mean we would have to have three people in one canoe and four people in the other canoe for the rest of the journey. This is not the best of arrangements in white-water, rapids. Usually you want to avoid overcrowding in the rapids.

We all looked in awe at the sheer rock walls and the huge house-sized boulders. Dave thought we should climb to the top of them and look down and see if we could see the lost canoe anywhere. Dave and I made the climb and worked our way upstream. To our amazement on the upstream side of the Narrows there was a little pool. In the pool were the canoe and the two oars going around in a mild circle. Once we climbed down, we noticed the center frame was a little bent but the canoe was still usable. We could not envision the power of the current at the Narrows and the strength of the cutback to pull a canoe with styrofoam floating devices underwater and upstream some 30 feet. Later we heard that if you get caught in that cutback you would be pulled under. The only way out is to grab the bottom of the river and try to pull your way out to the side. If you cannot crawl out that way you will be released in the pool where our canoe was five to ten minutes later. We were all very thankful that we narrowly escaped the Narrows.

Up to this point in our journey, the river was winning. Bill Kieffer kept asking if we were having fun yet. I did not know until another 100 yards down the river, that fifty-two-year-old Bill Kieffer had a heart problem and that his wife was very concerned about him going on this canoe trip. Apparently he also had a "War-woman Rapid" experience the night before. What else could go wrong?

One hundred yards after the Narrows is a class three, heart-pounding 6 foot vertical drop called Second Ledge. Again, our boaters had problems. Bill Kieffer was thrown from his canoe and landed on a rock, fortunately on his western hemisphere. He scrambled to the shore where he was going to regroup and check his heart rate. At this point, he met someone who was sunbathing. It was a very rude meeting with Bill's new friend slithering away from the party. Of course Bill wanted to call this little baby a rattle snake which is possible, and certainly sounds better for this story, but it could have been any one of a variety of snakes. There is a snake that is often mistaken for a poisonous snake and that is the northern water snake. Since the snake was on the Georgia side, we all concluded that it could not have been a Northern water snake. It could have been an eastern ribbon snake, or a copperhead, or an eastern hognose snake, but Bill is convinced it was a timber rattlesnake and since preachers never exaggerate, we will take him at his word.

At this point with one crash and burn after another, I realized that there was a good possibility that we might be late in getting the missionaries to all the families who had signed up to have them for dinner. Every family was excited to have a real missionary in their house to eat a meal missionaries never get: lasagna.

I told the group that since I was in the fastest craft I would go ahead of the group. I would go by myself and get to the cars and then to a country store to make a phone call to the church to let them know we might have to come straight to the conference service which was scheduled for 7:00. I also wanted the families to entertain the wives for dinner and to have the wives bring clothes for all the guys to change into at church. Don Clipperton especially would need a pair of pants for church, despite them being holy, they were still not appropriate for a mixed audience. Don was also on schedule to preach that night. I already knew I was not going to be home by 4:00 p.m. to help John with his bug project. It was a real shame too because I had seen bugs all over the river and was enamored with the number of Tiger Swallowtail butterflies that ruled the pools.

Without the map, I could only guess how far we were from the pullout. I took off ahead of the group and got real aggressive with the kayak for what seemed to be a couple of miles on the water. Then at the Eye-of-the-Needle I lost control of my boat and watched myself get ejected from its tomb to see the kayak actually go airborne and get lodged in between rocks while I kept my feet up and downstream. This was quite a ride as I floated through the rapids. The 75 foot-water-ride was so cold that it took my breath away. The headwaters for the Chattooga can be traced to rocky cliffs of Whiteside Mountain in North Carolina. Finally, I was dumped into a broad, deep, pool. The water was somewhat clear; I felt like Jonah in this big fish bowl. I was looking for Jaws, but only saw his cousins the redeye bass, the blue gill, the northern hogsucker, the river chub, the yellowfin shiner, the striped jumprock and the turquoise darter.

As I pulled myself up to a rock, I prayed and thanked God for preserving my life and I asked him to forgive me for my foolishness of canoeing alone ahead of the gang, not too smart. I then resolved in my heart that it would be better for us all to be a little late for supper than to be a little early for heaven. There I waited for about a half-hour until all the gang caught up with me. Once they arrived, they helped me recover my kayak from the Eye-of-the-Needle.

At this point, my confidence was a little shaken. I would portage around The Roller Coaster, a rodeo-like class three rapid. Everyone else shot the rapid and enjoyed it. Around the next bend, I again portaged escaping the Painted Rock, a class four rapid. The others again successfully shot the rapid. It was obvious, except for me, the team's navigational skills were getting better.

I was keeping my eye on my watch. It was already five o'clock. All day long I had been saying, "We are almost there – I know it!" Finally, we were almost there but I knew that we still would need to take precious time to go back to Earl's Ford and pick up Chuck's van and then drive back to Highway 76 to load the boats. After the scuttle runs we still would have an hour drive to get to church. At this point, with three more miles left, I knew we were not going to make it to anyone's house for dinner and that now it was going to be very close to even get to church by 7:00 p.m. for the service. As we went through the Hound's Tooth drop, I thought how appropriate for truly I would be in the doghouse tonight!

All day I had warned the guys of the infamous Bull Sluice that concludes Section III. The guys were exhausted and starving and by now were somewhat mutinous as I tried to bark navigational commands. The sun was coming down on the river and it was hard to see ahead in the sparkle and glare of the river.

What we could not see, we could hear. For the first time all-day, we heard an ominous roar downstream – Bull Sluice. Bull Sluice plunges 12 feet over a series of two back-to-back drops. The initial drop is over a curved ledge into a pool of powerful crosscurrents. Once you drop off the first ledge you land in a strong hydraulic that can easily flip your boat. Those who have been capsized and caught in the hydraulic and lived to tell about it have all said the same thing that it was like being flushed down a giant commode. I know that is somewhat crude, but apparently is the sensation.

Art Johns was also keenly aware of the danger of Bull Sluice. He wisely paddled ahead of us and climbed on top of the big half dome rock on the Georgia side. He was going to sound the alarm as the other boaters approached the Bull Sluice. There he waved his hands like a mad man and screamed, "The British are coming, the British are coming!" No, he did not say that. He bellowed, "Bull Sluice, everyone out of the river!" Art was heard at the last minute by the next boat in the line-up which was John Anderson and Don Clipperton's. They were able somehow to steer their canoe into a ridge of stones, a hydraulic parking space, in the fast-moving water. They were then going to get out of their canoe and follow-me on foot around the Bull Sluice. As Don Clipperton stepped out of the boat while John held it still, the weight shifted and with the lack of weight in the back, the canoe rose above the rocks holding it and took off with John. John was now on a solo flight heading straight for the Bull Sluice. Now if you live through the Toilet Bowl, the next danger is that the waters funnel wildly between a boulder pile and a large overhanging rock known as "Decapitation Rock." If one has a head there is no explanation needed as to why the rock is called "Decapitation Rock." Once through this supercharged chute of aerated water is a large recovery pool.

We all watched in horror as John floated away with the current. There was nothing we could do but pray. John, seeing the death trap in front of him, knew he had to abandon ship. He somehow maneuvered his body over the front of the canoe and jumped out of the craft just at the top of the Toilet Bowl. I thought he had a better chance of survival if he stayed in the boat and had at least the possibility of holding onto the canoe through the Sluice down to the recovery pool. Miraculously, John had the gymnastic ability to balance himself as he left the canoe and then to land upon a flat rock just under the surface on the brim of the fall. There sat John on the broken Toilet Bowl that continued to run with no hopes of jiggling the handle to shut off the fierce circular movement of water. John just sat there on the slippery rock.

It was now nearing 6:30 p.m. My fears were many. My first fear was how I was going to explain to Debbie Anderson that her husband was flushed down the Chattooga. Just several weeks prior to our trip there were two fatalities on the river. One death took place immediately below where John was precariously sitting. In fact, it took the rescue squad several days to get the body out of the hydraulics. This was running through my mind so I knew the best course of action was to somehow pull John off the rock from the backside and try to avoid him going through the Sluice at all costs.

It was now getting dark and another fear was setting in for John – hypothermia. We all had been wet all day and now with the sun setting it was getting cold. John was sitting in a few inches of rapid-fire water on a slippery rock. Could he hold on until we figured out a rescue plan? Could he avoid hypothermia in the process and where did he stand regarding his insulin for his diabetic condition?

The other two teams of canoes pulled ashore before the Sluice and portaged the Sluice on the Georgia side. The man-less canoe which John and Don abandoned at the sluice had conquered the Sluice and was floating in the recovery pool. I did notice that the frame of my canoe was severely bent and that the canoe was taking water. As I pulled it to shore I noticed a hole about the size of a half-dollar on its hull. I was glad that the craft had made it to its destination. It could not have gone any further without serious water problems. I knew I could duct-tape the hole when we got back home.

My biggest concern was how to extract John. All the missionaries brainstormed and Dave and Don thought that we could form a human chain from the South Carolina side and extend to John an oar to grab onto to pull himself towards us. We had no ropes, so the human chain would have to work. It took us about thirty minutes from the time John perched himself on the Sluice to get in position to rescue him from the middle of the river. I stayed below at the recovery pool just in case John slipped and came through the Sluice. The others created the necessary support team from above the Sluice.

The current was very strong as the men formed the chain. They inched towards the rock John was sitting on with the fear in mind that one slip and they all could go over the Sluice from the South Carolina side. I watched as John slowly stood and reached out to the extended oar that Don Clipperton offered him. John grasped it and slowly pulled himself upstream and over to the bank on the South Carolina side. We all cheered when it was clear that all links of the chain including John were going to live and not be broken!

We all gathered at the path that led up the hill to the parking lot where my River Rod was parked. I hardly had the strength to carry my kayak up the path. We had run on adrenaline all day and now were in great need of some food. We were all starving. Bill Kieffer asked for the fiftieth time during the trip, "Are we having fun yet?" We certainly had fun, but now I had the unpleasant task of calling the church and my wife to explain what had happened. It was now a little after 7:00 p.m. Needless to say, the opening night of the mission's conference would not have a single male missionary in attendance, nor the host pastor.

I knew that Allissa and all the church would be worried. Chuck had a cell phone so we tried to call the church but our efforts to connect were frustrated due to the fact we were out in the boonies where there were no towers aiding our cause. Later, I would find out that Allissa, at around 6:30 p.m. had called our assistant pastor and counseled that he better be ready to be the contingency plan since there was no sound or sight of the mission team. Skip would end up preaching an extemporaneous message that night. Everyone later said it was the best message he had ever preached. Don Clipperton's wife showed their slides of Argentina and then the church spent the rest of the evening in prayer for the lost – the lost missionaries.

Chuck and I in the meantime had to go to the start of our journey and pick up his van and then return to the parking lot where the mission team, boats and gear, were waiting. No one found any humor in my enquiry if they would like to go down Section IV of the Chattooga. It was only 9 miles in length with rapids called Screaming Left Turn, Rock Jumble, Seven Foot Falls, Corkscrew, Crack in the Rock, Jawbone, etc. Below Sock-em-dog was Dead Man's Pool. This is usually where one can find logs, limbs, bodies, styrofoam, lunches, drinks, shoes, oars and anything washed downstream. Then below that are Opossum Creek and finally the quiet Lake Tugaloo.

This section of the river is where the 1972 film Deliverance was filmed. There is one rock called "Deliverance Rock." I have never seen the film starring Burt Reynolds, Jon Voight, Ned Beatty and Ronny Cox, but have heard the music from the film, "Dueling Banjos." I knew I was going to need "Deliverance" when I got home. I was hoping I would still have a wife and a "job" when we got back to church. I was most thankful that all that ended up in Dead Man's Pool were Chuck's shoes, part of Don's pants, our Oreo cookies, one oar, one floating device, several bottles of Gatorade and one Chattooga map.

As we loaded the canoes and gear we prayed to thank the Lord for His mercy and safety. We then drove east and stopped at the first little store on the road where we devoured everything on their shelves. John Anderson drank an entire half-gallon of milk. I was able to call from the store but received no answer at church and could only leave a message on the answering machine hoping someone would pick it up. Allissa at about this time was talking with J. R. Nicholson about organizing a search party to find the lost missionaries. We got back in the car and continued to drive until we got to Walhalla where we stopped at Hardees. Again, we ate everything in sight. Again, I called the church. This time one of our members picked up the phone and finally we could reassure the church that all was well with the church's guests. Those who had remained at church were instantly given the message and there was a great sigh of relief and praise to God.

As we drove the last twenty minutes to the church from Walhalla I was bracing myself for the unknown currents at church and the "War Woman" rapids that I knew lurked ahead. We pulled into church at 9:00 p.m. hoping for a hero's welcome, which never came. We did make it, a little late, but all were alive. I begged Bill Heffley to stay by my side and to plead my case. Bill has a special way with my wife and I was going to need all the help I could get. I also was going to need Bill's help to assist in the delayed completion of John's massive bug project, which I promised that I would assist. After reuniting husbands to wives and explaining to those at the church the highlights from the day, Bill Heffley, and I walked home from the church, which was only one fourth mile down a dirt road. As I walked past Windsor's doghouse Bill made some untimely comments about where I would be sleeping that night.

Bill was able to find some strength through humor to stay awake as he helped Allissa label bugs. I needed toothpicks to keep my eyes open and was not much help on the project at 1:30 a.m. John was snoring. Allissa was not very amused with even Bill's best efforts to defuse the situation. The next day Bill would encourage Allissa to write out all of her husband's offences and the lessons that her husband needed to grasp from his trip down the Chattooga. Allissa would compile a list of twenty-one grievances. Bill would use some exceptional navigational techniques to steer our marriage away from "War Woman Rapids." For this I am eternally indebted. That night I dreamt of whitewater rapids spraying mist over the deck of my green torpedo. I had river on the brain and could not shut my mind down.

The next day at church I was confronted by a visit from an irate parishioner. She had her hands on her hips and asked me if I would ever grow up! I said with my mouth that I would attempt to grow up, but in my heart I knew that this was a little too much to ask of one's pastor. That day I met with some of the missionaries and begged them to cover for me with the deacons. They did a noble job and said they would do it all over again and that it was the greatest experience of their life! This helped, but the deacons wanted me to commit to them that I would not take the missionaries on such a dangerous expedition again. The following year we took the missionaries to a Christian bookstore called Noah's Ark to buy books. The deacons were happy with such a choice knowing that we were safe in the Ark.

On Tuesday night, we had our largest crowd show up for the mission's conference. Everyone wanted to hear what had happened. As I waited on the platform for the service to start, in came Missionary John Anderson on crutches and with a huge bandage on his head. He looked pitiful and needed two missionaries to drag him into the service. I knew that this was not going to be good PR for the conference, although it could be used to tug on heartstrings to support financially our endangered missionary friends. I watched aghast wondering if John had incurred all these injuries from the trip. Then all of John's accomplices and John began to laugh uncontrollably. They had set me up! We all howled breaking the tension in the air.

It was several days after the conference that I took my family and Bill Heffley to Clemson Outdoor Adventures where they sell kayaks. At the shop we talked to the owner and his wife about the various kayaks they had and which ones were designed for rivers like the Chattooga. In the conversation, they stressed how important it was to have the right kayak and equipment to navigate safely the Chattooga. Then the couple described what they had seen on a recent trip of theirs down the Chattooga. They described in detail how they came across a bunch of ill-prepared idiots at the Narrows on Section III of the Chattooga and tried to rescue their paddles, floating devices, drinks, etc. All I could do was force a smile and say, "Yea, bunch of idiots!"

The 1998 missionary conference at University Baptist Church is one that will never be forgotten. This story has literally circulated around the world. What a conference, Bill celebrated his sixty eighth birthday on the seventeenth of that week and was cured of his fear of water. Art Johns and Bill Kieffer would celebrate their fifty-third birthdays. My wife did not divorce me! Windsor eventually received his doghouse back. My kids wanted to hear the story over and over again! The deacons allowed me to continue to be the church's pastor, as long as I promised not to take missionaries down the Chattooga River, which I agreed to with my fingers crossed behind my back. The missionaries left with incredible financial support and later received a shirt that said, "I Survived UBC's Mission Conference."

THIS CHAPTER IS DEDICATED to the survivor's of the infamous Chattooga River ride: John Anderson, Don Clipperton, Bill Heffley, Chuck Horton, Art Johns, Bill Kieffer, and Dave Utter. The tenth year reunion was scheduled for October 12th, 2008. All parties were requested to meet at the

Bull Sluice prior to tackling Section IV. RSVP's were required.

Also, a big, hearty thanks goes to my Nephew Ryan Allen who has pestered me for five years to write this story. Love you Ryan, thanks for your motivation!

CHAPTER TWELVE

VISION FOR THE USE OF
TECHNOLOGY IN MINISTRY

How Technology will Affect management
for Sunday Morning preparation for Church

Each member of the church will be supplied with a computer that will have a built-in alarm that will be programmed to wake up each member with Pastor Senn's voice so that they will not oversleep and miss Sunday school. The computer will also play inspirational hymns in the morning and will have a short devotional from a DNA video dubbing of Charles Haddon Spurgeon. The screen will present the morning's Sunday school schedule and the church's bulletin. If unable to attend church that day, the church member will click on the attendance record for his Sunday school class and mark that he will be absent. If he is sick or needs prayer, this will be typed in so that the shepherd couple for his Sunday school class will be aware of it and have the class pray for him. Management will know immediately why so-and-so was absent from class bringing far greater accountability to the Sunday school program and a greater awareness of the personal needs of each church member. Management (i.e. Rick Robbins) will need to maintain a database for such record keeping as well as the programming of each week's web page for the current bulletin and announcements, etc.

How Technology will Affect the Management of the Sunday School Class

The Sunday school class will be hooked up to a satellite Sunday school program. This link will connect the local church to the Master Bible teachers in America (MBA), of whom Dr. Matthew Olson is one. Each class will have a satellite teacher who will thoroughly exposit God's Word on a big screen. Then the class shepherd will involve the class in discussion regarding the lesson using the study and discussion questions generated by the master teacher. If a student is absent, or sick at home, he can tune into the Master Teacher through the internet computer system.

If space is a problem for the local church, members can stay home during the Sunday school hour and simply interact via home computer with the Master Teacher's satellite class. Such classes via the Master Teacher's satellite program can also be taken for credit or audit and be counted for one's Bible degree. Those that take the class for credit would need to do homework and various projects that would be communicated to the satellite institute via the computer. The Sunday school manager/administrator will need to surf the net to find the best teacher for each class. There will be a measure of record keeping necessary for each class. Computer specialists and programmers will be needed to maintain a healthy Sunday school program. Each class will need at least one shepherding couple to keep the class somewhat personal and human.

How Technology will Affect the Management of the Morning Worship Service at 10:30 a.m.

The morning worship service will be affected greatly by technology. The worship management team will pre-plan each service coordinating the technology with the worship service. Each person in attendance will have a computer screen in his pew. On the screen will be a visitor's card and church information sheet for visitor's to fill out before, during or after the service. This information goes immediately into the visitor's/follow-up database. The computer screen will also have the church's web page accessible to inform the visitor of the many ministries in the church. Also, on the screen is the bulletin for that church service and a picture of each of our deacons and their geographic responsibilities divided by continents. This will save the cost and then some on the bulletins that "Starch" is requesting.

The music as well as the words for the service will be listed in the bulletin. The computer screen will have a screen available for the blind to read via Braille. The deaf will be able to read the words that the computer generates from the service.

If your guest does not speak English, then the computer can be programmed to translate church information into any language for them to read as well as to listen to when they desire. There will be headphones connected to the computer for those who want to hear the service and message in another language. They can quietly listen to the sermon or to the Denver Broncos game just as those who are hard of hearing can use the headphones to improve the quality of the sound of the service. Such services offered would need technicians and sensitive, AV men such as James Boyce, Tim Meenach, James Ferry, Seth Conable, Paul Bustamante, Peter Gordon and gadget gurus like Gary Oliver and Alan Upchurch.

Each person will have the sermon outline on his own screen. The sermon can be recorded and processed into a written text for those who would like to read along with the sermon with the bouncing ball. Such services can be downloaded onto their home computer, or a CD can be taken home after the morning service.

Shut-ins will be able to participate in the worship service of their local church via the Internet services of the home church. The worship service will show up on their screens at home. Shut-ins and those in the hospital will now be able to enjoy all current services and watch them live. This will be a great encouragement to them. They can also submit their prayer requests for their sickness, which will show up on the screen at the set times for prayer during the worship service. Also, such shut-ins could signify if they would like a visit or if they would like for the elders to visit to anoint them with oil and pray for them.

If the church is having auditorium space problems, then church members can be encouraged to stay home and watch the service. Another possibility would be for the overflow crowd to meet in the Fireside Chapel or another room on the church's campus to watch the service on either a big-screen or their own separate computer screens put in place for such observation and use.

Those on vacation or out camping could tune in to their home church's worship service. This would eliminate the difficulty of finding a church of like precious Internet on vacation and would allow the family not to feel like they missed anything at their home church. The missionaries that the church has sent out and who minister on a foreign field could tune in to the church services and feel right at home. They also could submit their prayer requests and progress from the week. Churches would no longer need to send tapes and videos to shut-ins, missionaries, etc. The monies saved could be used to purchase more technology to minister to the church family.

How Technology will Affect the Management of the Music Ministry at Tri-City Baptist Church

Pastor Larry Robbins would coordinate all the music with the electronic organs and other electronic instruments. Churches will no longer need an orchestra for the electronic keyboard and organ can reproduce such sounds very accurately and attractively. The key for success will be purchasing the proper sound system and equipment. Such electronic devices would pay for themselves over time since the local church would no longer need to hire any accompanists. The church music manager would need to understand the use of computers and electronic equipment.

Music would be led via the song leader with the hymnbook being on the hard drive of the computer and presented on the screen in the pew. This would eliminate the need of hymnbooks and the terrible expense of replacing them or worrying about people walking off with them. Also, you would not be distracted from your worship by the rustle of pages for the hymn would automatically come up on the screen. The song leader would no longer have to say, "Turn to #666 in your hymnbook." Young at Heart folks would be on the same page as the young folks and the bouncing ball on the screen would indicate which words and verses should be sung. No one would drop their hymnbook either. All church music would have the sound of professionally recorded church music. The small church would have the option of having a selection of choirs to choose from to program on the computer. Special music likewise could be piped in from any soloist in America or the world. This would eliminate the need for choir practices. Handel's *Messiah* could be played at Christmas without the need of extra choir practices. The quality of the music program will be highly professional. Additional monies will need to be spent on upgrading the church's sound system, speakers, etc. so that nothing is lost in the transmission of the electronic technology.

In addition to technology improving the music program, young children could be entertained during the worship service via the computer. Management would need to develop further Bible computer games and puzzles for kids to play. This will eliminate much of the wiggle-worm distractions in the service and kids with Attention Deficit Disorders will be ministered to since computer games have a medicinal affect on those who have the highly contagious ADD.

How Technology will Affect the Offerings at Tri-City

During the service, an electronic offering will be taken. Churches will take Visa and Master Card. Those worshiping or visiting can swipe their card down the side of the computer which would have the financial set-up for handling such trans-actions. For church members (i.e. Tom and Kim Hurst) an automatic deduction from their paycheck will be arranged. This will eliminate a lot of paper work and make one's giving easy to track. The church would immediately electronically receipt your gift via email/internet to confirm the transaction. The offerings would go on to the church's database as well as emailed to the IRS as a tax-deduction. This will be required by the IRS if you would like your charitable contribution to be tax deduct-ible. This process would allow the IRS to confirm your Income Tax figures with your actual giving. This will save much paper work and expense for both the church and for E & E Block. Also, the church will have greater stability financially knowing when each member's automatic deductions will take place as well as the amount.

If members want to contribute to the church on a special offering, building project, etc. a church debit card would be used. Such electronic offerings would eliminate the need of Bill Honaker and Dick Vose looking all over the church for the offering plates and the need of ushers who are constantly dropping the plates or making change for donors.

Since an offering could be taken literally in a second, offertories would not be needed, although that could be perceived by some as being too cold. In lieu of regular offerings and offertories as we know them, the church could have what could be called a memorial offering, where folks could meditate on what they have given, or not given. Also, the offertory could be used to give some reluctant givers the oppor-tunity to reconsider swiping their credit card. This would be exceptionally convict-ing if the message appeared on the screen with their annual giving record and the last time they gave to a charitable organization. Bible verses on giving could be scanned across the screen during the offertory or even pictures of one's missionaries minister-ing to the hungry, balding and sick. To make the plea more personal, the missionary could interact with the pew sitter and stress his needs and plead his case.

For more information on how to successfully plead for monies, confer the web-site called fortmill@tbaker. This process in taking offerings will affect manage-ment greatly in the local church. Deacons, treasurers, Doug Scheetz, Ched Miller, Janine Yurka, Karen Price, Nathan Drake, etc. will not have to miss services counting money or arranging times to meet to count and deposit monies. There will be no need of a security system or a safe to hold monies in the church. No one will need to follow the deacon's wives to the bank to assure a safe deposit. The financial record keeping will be greatly simplified as a result of direct deposits and debit card use.

How Technology will Affect Sunday Worship at Tri-City

The technology described thus far relates to the Lord's Day. The management burden will fall mostly on the computer technicians in the church and the various department heads such as the Sunday School Directors, Music Directors, Worship Directors, Pastors, etc. The key will be good communication and coordination between them and the Web-Masters. Technology will improve greatly the quality of communication between member and home church, missionary and home church, shut-in and home church, visitor and home church, etc.

Technology will reduce the workload for the modern-day priests on the Lord's Day. The giving process as previously stated will minimize the financial workload needed on the Lord's Day. The music ministry will be enhanced by technology only to the degree that the local church is comfortable with the artificial choirs, artificial orchestras, and artificial special music. Management will have to make a decision between a quality music program and a more personal, human program. Sunday school will be taught by the theological experts and national guns, rather than the Bubba who butchers the King's English in his Scofield Bible. This will reduce the workload for the Sunday school department and its teachers. In fact, technology will be so helpful that the majority of the church family on the Lord's Day could stay home and watch the service of their home church and feel like they only missed some of the people. Church could potentially become more of a spectator's sport.

The seeker sensitive pastor will need to warn his church family on the screen from time-to-time of this peril. The competition between churches would not be seen in church jumping, but in Internet jumping. Church members will be tempted to scan the Internet to find other church services that they could observe. These services will offer incentives for people to interact on their computer and to email addresses and numbers to get free information about their ministry. It could be that some members of your church could hypothetically become members over the Internet with hundreds of other churches around the country and world. In fact, such a process would give new meaning and application to the Bible's teaching on the universal church.

The Internet could be used greatly in church-planting efforts. New members could easily be attained over the net. However, it is my opinion the Local church will be overshadowed by the preeminence of a one-world church. Members of this one-world church will be able to receive daily messages over the Internet from the spokesman of their glamorous church. The world will be able to enjoy the services of such a lamb.

Such communication will allow Tower of Babel Ministries to have a world-wide scope. It is interesting that the former builders of Babel had communication down to a science. The people were on-line with one another, had clear goals established and shared ownership in the project. The key ingredient to the potential success of any Babel is communication. The 21st century church will make great strides in communication that will enhance unity. The sweet-spirited-lamb of the Tower of Babel Ministries will have both the old and new tools to use to unify his efforts. The city cradled by the peaks of Aventine, Caelian, Capitoline, Esquiline, Palatine, Quirinal and Viminal will be ultimately the beneficiary of such communication systems. There will be no mystery that the fatherly leader of Tower of Babel Ministries will use the world's technology to its fullest. Such ministries will be aided by benevolent political leaders who will admire the church's desire to have a global ministry via technology.

How Technology will Affect Faith Baptist Christian School

The Greenville News (Thursday, November 30, 2000) stated that we are going through an "e-commerce revolution" which needs "a steady supply of professionals who are well-versed in the technical and managerial aspects of e-commerce." Today the Internet accounts for 3.8 million jobs, according to a recent study by the University of Texas Center for Research in Electronic Commerce. It is expected to generate $500 billion in revenue by the end of 2000. Close to 400,000 e-commerce jobs were created in 1999.

One area of business that is being cultivated over the Internet and via satellite is education. Today, the church has many educational options. One that is growing is the use of satellite and the Internet to receive an education. Today there are some twenty to thirty e-commerce degree programs in America. David Grigsby, Clemson University's director of the graduate business program said, "The greatest unmet needs are among a very large group of business professionals who received their undergraduate degrees prior to the e-commerce revolution and who now find themselves lacking the technical knowledge needed for professional advancement." Such educational advancements will be met by technology for those who would like to advance from kindergarten, high school, college or a Ph.D. program.

For the local church and her families, technology will greatly affect the management of the Christian Day School. Schools will be able to get on-line with satellite schools that have the crème-of-the-crop as their teachers. This will eliminate the need of hiring qualified teachers at the local level. Schools will only need to hire workers to monitor the classes. Most of the paper work will be done over the Internet including the grading of most projects. Records will be maintained by a database hooked up to each satellite school. Again, school and church staff can be reduced by such technological advances. In fact, most schooling will be based out of the home rather than the Christian school. This will reduce the need of building educational facilities. Another savings will come from the savings of not needing to transport students to school. All these savings can potentially lead to higher contributions to the local church through the personal debit card, which can amount to greater technological tools being purchased.

Technology will affect greatly the Christian Day School with more and more of her students being home schooled via technological gains in education. It will be cheaper to be home schooled. The materials and teachers that they will have at home will be the best e-money can buy. School administrators will need to adjust their plans for their schools greatly. In fact, they may need to look for another source of employment themselves. One of the options would be for them to take an e-mail class on computers and technology and consider starting their own satellite Internet school. Such schools will need to have good administrators. Ultimately, technology will produce a public state Internet school that would compete on a state level, which would later conform to a national standard and then a worldwide level. Education will be unified and standardized by technology, so that every American will have equal access to the same education that their tax and lottery money generates.

For the Christian school manager, he will need to be sensitive to the fact that education is going to shift from traditional settings to the home computer. This will take place at all academic levels. Colleges need to be prepared to adjust to the growing interest in e-studies at home. There will be fewer students actually attending our campuses except for special conferences and technological upgrade meetings. This will affect Pastors Ted Rich, Brandon King and Sergio Ramirez and the members of Cross Impact Campus Ministries. Whereas 85 per cent of Pastor Rich's ministry is done via email now, it will become 99 per cent of his future ministry. It would be best to invest in a new control center for his e-campus ministry. Schools will need to invest more and more into technology to remain competitive with other schools. Competition will not be at the publishing house level, but at the Internet level.

The Christian school manager must also plan to see a major restructuring of the educational grade system. Children will be starting school earlier and will be learning at such a fast pace via electronics that the average age for the graduate of high school will be reduced to twelve. The majority of college students will graduate by the time they get their driver's license at age sixteen. No one will be able to apply for a driver's license unless they have a college degree. These age changes for high school and college will have a huge impact on the school systems as well as the workforce.

Technology will improve the athletic competition between various home schools and Christian schools. Instead of competing on the field with sports such as soccer, basketball, baseball, etc., sports will be played over the Internet. This will give great parity to both the small and large schools as well as for the individual home-schooler who wants to compete at a national level.

The development of a virtual reality sports setting will allow each person competing to realize their sports fantasies. The result would be that no one would ever lose, unless they chose that outcome, no one would get physically or emotionally hurt, and no Christian players would ever hurt their testimony on the court.

Virtual reality sports would do much for building one's self-esteem and would help parent each student's inner child. All children could participate and receive the well-rounded experience of academics and sports. Again, after the initial technological expense of the virtual reality sports equipment, the educator would have a sports program that would need minimal financial input. Imagine the savings for the school, no referees to pay, no facilities to build, and no college gymnasiums that could be used for filming *Hoosiers II* to be renovated. Once again, technology will save Christian schools and colleges money in the long run.

How Technology will Affect Communication for Tri-City's church staff meetings

There is no doubt that the church without a website will be like a church without a steeple. Churches will need to have a Web-master like Alan Upchurch. After hiring a pastor, the second man will no longer be the youth pastor (Pastor Durrill) or the music man (Pastor Robbins) or the YAH-YAH pastor (Pastor Taylor), but the Web Master-Pastor. Bible Colleges will need to incorporate in their program the training for Web Pastors. The first step in this process is to have college administrators assign pastors in their D-min programs papers such as, *"How will technology affect management in the Next Decade."* From there, courses will be designed for the Web Pastor and four years from now we will have Web Pastor Clones marching in May. These Web Pastors will then be hired by the local church to design websites for their local churches that are attractive and informative. The web page will be used to promote the local church and to communicate the church's doctrine, programs, missionaries, etc. Each missionary of the local church will also be equipped with email capability and will be able to communicate daily with their sending and supporting churches.

Computers will be greatly improved to the point that typing will be made practically obsolete by the computer being able to recognize voices and words and then transform them into text on the computer. Once the text is on the screen, the sophisticated grammar check will kick-in to clean up the text. Mary Vose will be able to edit the pastor's ridiculous books, like, *Colorado Snow* by the use of voice commands. This will greatly enhance the publication of e-books. Improvements in technology will include wireless computer and phone systems and improved high-resolution computer screens. Such displays will be easier to read than your standard book. Digital books will be the trend of the future, with hard copies and bound books stored away in museums for future generations to gawk at. Such generations will be greatly amused as to how the Pre-E culture read books.

The IBM *Selectric II* will be replaced with each staff member being equipped with first a Palm-operated computer system, which acts as their day-timer. These digital microcomputers will assist management. Later, this system will be replaced by a wrist watch system that operates by voice recognition and other commands. Each staff member will be supplied with a digital phone. This device will be later incorporated into the wristwatch system and will be operated by computerized vision implants. The ultimate development of the computer system and phone system will be incorporated into various chips that will be implanted under the skin so that one does not have to run the risk of losing their e-watch or damaging it. Also such chips will be wonderfully used to locate church members via satellite search. If a church member ceases to log on to e-church, the administrator can trace the backslider by a satellite search. This will assist churches in finding those church members and visitors that seem to disappear so suddenly. Such a device will assist the E-Pastor in knowing the state and whereabouts of his flock. At membership, such chips could be upgraded with e-church bites that automatically signal when such a member slips into inappropriate places or into sins that would be harmful for them. Such accountability would reduce Internet pornography problems with members, etc.

To keep things personal for the E-pastor, technology will produce a phone system that allows him to have a feature on his computer phone screen that can be turned on to see his members and for them to see him. This will produce greater accountability between E-pastor and E-member. The pastor will really wonder if one of his members does not turn on their screen. The need of turning on the screen will produce greater conviction in the lives of church members and a desire to live a more holy life. As with most of technology it can be used for good or for bad. There will be the temptation of some church members to have a specially designed video that they plug in when the pastor calls that has them sitting at their desk, with an open Bible and a half-empty coffee mug. There are no doubt some risks and liabilities with the picture phone, but it would be hard to imagine mankind using it to promote licentiousness. On the most part, the benefits of the picture phone will far outweigh the liabilities. Some immediate benefits of tele-conferencing come to mind: Churches will be able to see their missionaries on the foreign field; new converts can be introduced and interviewed; ordination councils could include the pastors who could not travel the distance to see their preacher boy ordained; grandparents will be able to watch their grand babies take their first steps right before their very eyes, etc.

How Technology will Affect Church Visitation

Each EE-church will have a multi-cultural, church staff due to "electronic immigration." Geographic borders potentially could become obsolete as "electronic immigration" assists expansion in global missions. Imagine on church visitation that a family in your church meets a family from India. Such a family could have a visit with an Indian Pastor. Churches will be equipped with desk-top video-conferencing equipment that will allow for the E-pastor/missionary living in India to have a "virtual visit" with the new contact to one's local church. In fact, much of church visitation will be able to be done through e-mail to e-mail visitation, rather than door-to-door visitation. Church visits will be accomplished through "virtual visits."

Hospital visitation for the church staff will be reduced through the use of surrogate doctors and other professionals. Medical technology will assist people in living longer and healthier. There will be less pollution. Gene therapy will reduce diseases. It will not be unusual to see many octogenarians maintaining their contribution in the work place. The age of retirement will be raised to seventy and above. Management will need to think through more carefully their retirement benefit plans, because the average age of people will push closer to eighty. Blue-collar workers will make up only a small percentage of the workforce, perhaps 10 per cent or less. Computer education will become even more vital for survival and success. From farms to Farmall tractors computers will be used and needed. Chickens will be able to produce scrambled eggs directly via computer chips; cows will be programmed to produce not only white milk, but also chocolate milk via special udder programming. Such innovative products will be marketed via e-sales.

The prison ministry will take on some new changes. With sensors and computer chips implanted within criminal's bodies, they will be paroled and will be able to be traced at any time of day. This will reduce subsequent murders and robberies.

Children who receive demerits, detentions at school, or who are considered "At-Risk" children will receive computer implants to monitor their activity. All crimes will be easily traced to the criminal. Drug abuse will be filtered with such computer chips and will alert global police of one's misconduct. Such technology will affect ministries that deal with drug and alcohol treatment.

Our benevolence ministries that assist people in paying their bills and especially their electrical bills will be reduced due to new technology that deals with self-contained generators in our homes that use fusion as a means of supplying power to our appliances. The ultimate generator will be the human body's metabolism, which will fuel our personal computers. As long as people have a metabolism, they will at least be able to run their personal computer systems. The key ministry as it will relate to benevolence ministries is to keep people on-line and upgraded. People will be visiting our churches and expressing their needs of computer upgrades so that they can survive and provide for their children the virtual Christmas of their dreams. Upgrades will become the key issue in managing people. Church management will need to develop specific ministries for the Yuppy Upgrades, as well as those who are on the other end with Lowgrades. The majority of our ministry will still be with the Middle-grade people. Such new classifications of the classes will be needed to design properly effective ministries for all.

How Technology will Affect Faith Promise Missions

Missionaries who use a slide presentation with a carousel will be considered out-dated and obsolete. Power-point presentations will be the trend and digital camera work will permit videos and still pictures to be incorporated into video presentations via the computer system. Missionaries will be able to present their work in a more effective way to the congregation and will be able to maintain communication with supporters via email and the Internet. This will eliminate most of the postage expense normally associated with missions. Communication will be instantaneous from any point of the world.

A one-world e-currency will eliminate the missionary's hassle to convert currencies. Checks will not need to be mailed, but will be electronically deposited. Local churches will be assisted by the mission board to route electronically their support e-checks directly to the missionary. This will eliminate long waits for money for the missionary and give the missionary the much-needed cash flow to do ministry.

Technology will develop an anti-Babel device that converts one's speech and language into the foreign language of their choosing. This will minimize the need of missionaries needing to go to language school. This device will be called the *Pentecost II*. Not only will this device convert audibly one language to another, but can also do a hard copy of the process on the computer screen. Missionaries will benefit greatly by such technological devices. Not only will this device be able to speak any language in the world, but can be dialed in regionally to get your regional accents in any set language. This would allow Southerners to understand Northerners, and Westerners to understand Easterners and vice versa, and all to understand the likes of Andrew Sidles.

How Technology will Affect future Weddings and Funerals at Tri-City

Technology will do much for e-courting. The management issue of dating versus courting will be resolved with e-courting. There will be a national database developed from each person's implanted computer chip with all the vital information necessary for proper matchmaking. Couples will be introduced via the Internet and by live pictures on the phone screen. No longer will pictures need to be exchanged or photos of Fido be mailed due to tele-conferencing. E-courting will be the trend of the future for the church.

There will be an Andy Griffith filter that screens out all unsaved and inappropriate applicant interviews. Parents will automatically be emailed the potential e-match so that they can screen out those they do not feel comfortable with and be able to be involved in the process from the beginning. The Andy Griffith filter will prevent the unmarried from accessing their e-match until their parents give parental consent to unveil the screen. With parental permission, e-weddings could be accomplished in a virtual reality marriage ceremony. This would save the families enormous wedding and transportation expense and will allow them to spend the money on technological gifts for the newlyweds. Newlyweds would have the option of living together or living apart but communicating via email. In most churches there always seems to be a handful of single people who are not able to meet Mr. E-man or Miss

E-woman. This scenario will be greatly challenged by E-conferences for the single church member. The Internet will help the E-Pastor by providing him a national and international resource to use to assist in ministering to the single folks in his church.

Technology in America will improve the way funerals are conducted. Some funeral homes are adding drive-through funeral services where family and friends can simply drive-through and view their loved one in a display casket.

Rather than sending flowers to the family, friends can send e-cards which will last longer than the flowers and will be cheaper. Monies saved could be designated for the one's e-charity of their choice. Ideally, church members would select only separated e-charities.

Pastors will have to deal more and more with the issue of cremation and the sensitive process of removing computer chips from the deceased. Most family members would not want strangers digging up such chips since such chips would contain a digital, video record of one's life that could be plugged in and screened. Obviously, one would not want such chips to fall into the wrong hands without some serious editing. One would not want them to fall into the wrong hands even with serious editing! What worse could happen, when a man's chips are down than for someone to take advantage of him and get into his cyberspace?

There will be no need to write biographies or autobiographies with such devices implanted that record all of life's ups and downs. Such implants will also act as a medical "dip-stick" that can give early warnings to any cancer cells or life threatening conditions developing in the body. There will be no more need of graveyards or graveside services. Ashes will be kept by the family, and an e-cemetery will be created on the Internet that maintains the computer chip of the deceased.

CONCLUSION

Technology and especially the computer chip will be a management issue for churches to consider and evaluate. There will be many benefits derived by the use of such chips. For parents one benefit would be that you would be able to locate your children at any time or place. Instead of the slogan, "Have you hugged your child today?" The question would be better-worded, "Have you surfed for your child on the Internet today?" Not only could the chip be used to locate your children, but also could be used as a tool to assist one's financial record keeping. In fact, a neat idea would be to use these implanted chips as your identification mark for all transactions. This would eliminate consumer fraud with credit cards. One would not need to fear being robbed. The only danger would be for one-armed bandits to rob others of both limb and chip. That is not a very pleasant thought and one we need not worry ourselves with today. It would be hard to imagine how man could abuse such a system with such implants either in their right hand or in their foreheads. It seems almost fool-proof.

An ethical question that church management will need to address is where does one draw the line with computer implants and biotechnology? Bran Ferren of Walt Disney Imagineering stated in the *New York Times* that, "technology needed for an early Internet connection implant is no more than twenty-five years off. Imagine that you could understand any language, remember any joke, solve any equation, get the latest news, balance your checkbook, communicate with others, and have near-instant access to any book ever published, without ever having to leave the privacy of yourself."

At present millions of medical devices are implanted in humans each year. These include pacemakers, blood vessel replacements, hip joints, eye lens implants, drainage tubes, heart valves, etc. The body reacts funny to these "foreign objects." The goal will be to create an implant that interfaces with the human body where the body responds "naturally" to them. These present implants are a tremendous help to their recipients. Again, the question is, where does one draw the line when it comes to the Human Genome Project and the development of artificial intelligence? How much gene therapy in the womb is healthy, or repairs to fractured DNA? In Genesis chapter six the human race was being tampered with by the union of the *"sons of God"* with the *"daughters of men."* Such unions were producing *"giants in the earth."*

The end result of angels and man transgressing their natural limits was further corruption and then worldwide judgment.

Fortunately, with modern-man's progress it is hard to envision him today using technology in a way that would harm or corrupt mankind. Dr. Darren Dawson, a Clemson professor who teaches computer engineering and robotics, is encouraged with the progress in developing a virtual reality world and robots that will have all the earmarks of a human being. Through his research and technology he has cultivated such an image that is called the NICOLAI COSTESCU – 666, which presently is capable of speaking both English and Romanian. The last frontier for the scientist is the issue of how to give life to such a creature and to future images. At present, no form of life has been able to be injected into such creatures by science. It is amazing that man can fashion the NICOLAI - 666; however, it appears that life itself will need to come from outside the realm of technology. Likewise, we must keep in mind that true church life can only come from God and not from any other source, including technology.

I am deeply encouraged by the technological vision that our church staff and deacons share with me. The future will rest in Pastor Taylor's ability to open up his Windows and to receive e-mail communication. In the year 2004, we will take the next step to a virtual reality church by using e-mail to communicate with our church family. Some are ready for this leap of faith, others are still not sure what e-mail is, but regardless we are going to go on-line. We will send this document to all our faithful e-mailers and prepare them for future technological recommendations. We are taking one small step for Technology, one giant step for Tri-City Baptist Church. Today truly marks a new e-ra.

THIS CHAPTER IS DEDICATED to several of my computer friends. **First, I dedicate this chapter to Dan "Gates" Wooster who purchased for me my first computer: a 286 Dan-dy. Over the years, we have upgraded. The Woosters were the first easterners to visit us in Denver. They arrived the day after we pulled into the driveway with our Frank-Johnson-operated-U-Haul. I would like to think that Dan traveled 1,600 miles just to set up my wireless computer network in my home office. Thanks for all your help over the years Dan!**

ALSO, THIS CHAPTER IS DEDICATED to Nicolae Costescu, Ian Gravagne, Gary Oliver, Andy Broadworth, James Boyce, Wayne Simon, Tim Meenach, Alan Upchurch, and all my computer guru friends for all of their computer help over the years. They all know that I am computer illiterate and have come to my aid on many an occasion!

CHAPTER THIRTEEN

THE MYSTERIES OF THE PARCO INN

This fictional story is dedicated to the workers of the Baptist Youth Mission, the Heart and Home families and the young folks who come to live at the Parco Inn in Sinclair, Wyoming.

Danny was awakened when he heard the train whistle at 2:11 a.m. He was angry at first for he was exhausted and needed the sleep. He also had to wake up early to help James Mueller with the garbage detail. In another room was Amanda, she too was wakened by the blast. She tossed and turned and tried to go back to sleep but was too scared to shut her eyes.

The next morning Danny and Amanda asked Rod Anderson why the train engineer was so thoughtless as to sound his whistle at such a time in the morning. The question made Rod and Faith extremely uncomfortable. With some hesitation, Rod began to explain why every night at 2:11 a.m. the train whistle sounded.

The story he told went back to the "roaring 20's." General Grenville M. Dodge had an engineer named Timmy "the hammer" Tutton. He was the engineer of the Union Pacific train #25561, nicknamed the "Iron Horse" by Chief "Heath Bar." Timmy "the hammer" would tank up with North Platte water at the Rawlins station. Every morning he would then gurgle through the little Rag Town at 2:11 a.m. At first, it was not his practice to blow the whistle at 2:11 a.m. In fact, he tried to let the refinery men and their families sleep. It would not be until Friday night,

145

August 13th that "the hammer" would make it his daily practice to blow the whistle at 2:11 a.m.

What happened on Friday, August 13th, 1924? Whitney Anderson could tell you! It was an exceptionally windy night in the town that was moving forward from Rags to Riches because of Highway 30 and the new oil refinery called the Producers And Refiners Corporation. Its initials were PARCO, hence the new name for the town. That night Mr. Frank Kistler was hosting a party at the Parco Inn for his baseball team, the Oil Cans. The team had just finished their season with a 16-4 record. They had just beaten the Hanna Whitesocks coached by Mark White. The final score was 3-2, a very satisfying victory in front of 1,500 people sitting in the freshly painted grandstand. "Squeaky" Joe Harman was the winning pitcher. As a hurler for the Oil Cans, he was known for his heat! Mike "Bubba" Durrill led the team in homeruns as well as strikeouts. He used a bat that was made of petrified wood from Medicine Bow. With one swing of "Old Lightning" he hit a towering home run in the bottom of the eighth to give the Oil Cans the lead. The real hero of the game, however, was Oil Can's "Slick Willy." With the bases loaded in the ninth he made the game-saving catch in left field when he snagged a frozen rope that was destined for Love's Theatre to end the game. The team, all but for "Bubba," carried "Slick Willy" off the field on their shoulders. "Bubba" hated old "Slick Willy" and had complained on many occasions to his coach. He told Coach Wright repeatedly that he wanted to kill old "Slick Willy." The coach always countered by telling him what was right. His constant message for "Bubba" was to put off such hatred!

At the party "Slick Willy" was enjoying the attention of Oil Can Serenaders "Goldie Locks." This was not a good thing for "Goldie Locks" was married to Dave Cogswell the biggest, meanest brick-maker in Wyoming. He had allegedly chewed off the ear of a man who simply winked at "Goldie Locks." Now "Slick Willy" was doing the Charleston with "Goldie Locks." This was a big mistake in the west; he would have been far safer doing the Cheyenne. Fortunately for "Slick Willy," the party was interrupted when a circuit-riding preacher by the name of Mike "Sawdust" Holmes entered the main lobby. He was in town to preach at the little Community Church that was ironically presented to Parco by the wife of Mr. Frank Kistler, Florence Marie. She also had given the church a beautiful Oxford King James Bible. The irony was this, while Frank was at the Parco Hotel drinking with his team, she was home preparing her heart for the next day, the Lord's Day. Preacher Mike "Sawdust" Holmes told Frank and the Oil Cans that it was time to call it a night, that it was past curfew and that folks in town needed to get some rest before the Lord's Day. The room got awfully quiet after "Sawdust's" announcement. Then "Slick Willy" started to mock the Baptist preacher and said, "Go up, ye bald head, go up!" Well that is something Ole "Slick Willy" should have never said. The evangelist stood his ground and said, "Slick Willy, tonight I am going to pray that God will judge you by a she-bear!" Then he paused and said, "And, I don't mind putting feet to my prayers." Then "Sawdust" stomped out of the Parco Inn.

Well this put a damper on the party to say the least. The team then quietly checked into their rooms. "Slick Willy" checked into room 211. "Bubba" who was still angry with "Slick Willy" and jealous that "Slick Willy" had slain his ten thousands checked into the adjoining room.

A strong wind rattled the windows. It was 2:11 a.m. when neighbors heard Bimbo, a red healer mix, barking followed by a scream within the Parco Inn. As the crowd gathered in the ballroom of the Parco Inn, they stared at "Slick Willy" whose limp body floated in the fountain. There was a hand-written message that was posted to the buffalo head on the wall with an arrow. It simply and sacrilegiously said, "To the one who has been eating my porridge, great catch, now be baptized and meet your Maker!"

Rod then said to Danny, "The coroner noted the time of "Slick Willy's" death as 2:11 a.m. Oddly that was his batting average as well as the room that he had checked into that evening. From that day forward, the engineers on the trains have blown the whistle at 2:11 a.m. in memory of that tragic evening. Oddly, the story does not end there. I would like to tell you more but we all need to get to work. Mr. Tim Demoret is waiting to start teaching English." Danny then said, "I will go to class, but first tell me, who killed "Slick Willy?" Rod then said, "Well that is a mystery! Who do you think killed "Slick Willy:" the preacher, Bubba, or Mr. Cogswell?"

After a day of hard work on April 26, 2005 at the Parco Inn, the work team from Ft. Pierce, Florida gathered in the main lobby and gazed at the weathered buffalo head above the fireplace. Katie had earlier been in the room and had the odd feeling that she was not alone. She had the eerie feeling that someone was watching her. As she walked around the room her eyes caught the eyes of the buffalo. At first, she thought she was seeing things. It was her perception that the eyes of the buffalo were following her every movement. Then to her horror the eyes of the buffalo turned bright red for what seemed like an eternity. She quickly ran to her room to get Rene. Rene teased her unmercifully about seeing things. Now the whole group looked curiously at the buffalo.

Faith Anderson was meeting with the girls to tell them about some of the history of the Parco Inn. Katie asked Mrs. Anderson if anyone had ever seen the eyes of the buffalo turn red. At that point little Annie Anderson, said, "It is a sign." Mrs. Anderson's face then turned red. She asked Katie, "Who told you about the story of the little girl Sarah?"

Katie said, "What story, Sarah who?" Mrs. Anderson hesitated, but realized that the group's curiosity had more potential for harm than the story itself. Alyssa Anderson said, "Tell them mom, they need to know." Mrs. Anderson then went on to tell the tragic story of Sarah, plain and short.

It was on Halloween, October 31, 1926, when the Parco Inn was hosting a banquet in honor of the city's special guest, Amelia Earhart. The mayor of Parco, Art Genzler, was in attendance as well as Wyoming Senator Doug "Starch" Sheets. The ballroom was exquisitely decorated. The menu included fresh lobster cocktail Neptune, salted almonds, hearts of celery, cream of chicken croutons soufflé, minions of Sandabs au Beuere, Pommes De Terre A l'Julienne, punch De Parco, red licorice, filet mignon pyramid and roast milk-fed turkey with chestnut dressing Bar Le Duc, salad epicure, parisienne potatoes, cheese straws, petit fours and café noir.

All the guests were dressed in Halloween costumes. The most common costumes were Spanish cavaliers, toreadors, matadors, and senoritas. Other outfits included Arab sheiks, Chinese Buddhas, headless horsemen, Avalanche hockey players, old people dressed as young people and vice versa. It was described as "the greatest international setting ever witnessed in Carbon County."

The town was buzzing with excitement especially when Amelia flew into town in her Beech-nut, four-passenger Lockheed-Vega plane with a 520 horsepower Wasp motor. She and her guest, the highly decorated Colonel Tyson Schrecengost had just flown in from Detroit. Mayor Genzler presented her with a silver teaspoon engraved with the words, "Parco Inn." In the audience was a young couple dressed as George and Martha Washington. Their real names were John and Bonet Temporal. They had a six-year old daughter by the name of Sarah. They had checked into the Parco Inn the day before and had received their keys to room 211. They were on vacation and regrettably had brought with them their daughter Sarah. This was because at the last minute their babysitter had come down with chicken pox. Sarah was already feeling bad because her mother had told her that she did not wish for her to come and that she always ruined their plans. Sarah was still trying to overcome her mother's words that she did not love her and that she wished that she was never born. It was confusing to Sarah why her father did not come to her aid when her mother yelled at her and pulled on her hair. Fortunately, she did not know that he was not her biological father. Sarah's true father was a wrangler by the name of Levi. John's attitude towards Sarah was less than supportive. He despised the little girl and was reminded of the wrangler every time he looked into her face. His heart was full of bitterness towards Bonet and was still unable to forgive her for her unfaithfulness. They were hoping that this vacation could help them move forward, but they were not making much progress.

As the couple was getting ready for the costume party and banquet in honor of Amelia Earhart, Sarah begged to go with them. She wanted to dress up as Cinderella and join them in the ballroom. Angrily her parents had said no and that she was going to stay in her room all night. She cried but her tears were of no avail. Instead of comfort, she received a slap to the face. She was commanded to stop crying and informed that she would be staying in her room for the evening. Little Sarah had already learned that if she continued to cry that she would be yanked and pulled and slapped further. She rubbed her swollen red eyes and dragged herself to her room. Inside her room she could hear the laughter, the music, the singing that rose above the balcony of the mezzanine. Such noises flowed between the floors of the Inn and were amplified by the heat registers in the hallway. Sarah finally cried herself to sleep holding her stuffed teddy bear.

At this point, Faith Anderson paused. Katie Anderson said, "Mom, tell them the rest of the story!" Faith hesitated and then she continued to explain that several of the guests had reported to the manager of the Parco Inn that Halloween night, how they had noticed the eyes of the Buffalo had turned red for a few seconds. The manager tried to downplay such phenomena and explained that it was really the red wine that was creating such effects.

At 2:11 a.m. the party was still going strong. Witnesses later said that it was about 2:00 a.m. when they last saw George and Martha Washington. One witness noticed that the couple had not danced together all night and that Mrs. Washington was a frequent guest to the Parco Punch. The only person she danced with was a blacksmith masquerading as Benedict Arnold. When interviewed later by Parco's chief of police, Jeff Sanders, the couple said they were taking a walk outside and were sitting on the ledge of the water fountain in the square when the scream was heard. It was a very strange night, the wind had picked up and the windows rattled, then there was the barking of Parco, a red healer mix named after the town. Then there was a thud, then screams, and then the music abruptly stopped. There on the floor of the fireplace room was the lifeless body of six-year old Sarah Temporal who allegedly fell off the balcony straining to see and to find her parents.

Pioneer woman, Kristine, then quickly asked, "Did she accidentally fall or did her father or mother push her over the edge?" Faith then said, "We don't know, it is one of the mysteries of the Parco Inn." Faith then went on to explain that Mr. Temporal's cloak was found in the empty room when the police went to find the couple to tell them their daughter had died. This was the only evidence that at least Mr. Temporal had returned to the room before her death, but it was not conclusive evidence to charge him.

Whitney, then interrupted her mom and said that she had learned something very strange at her work at the library about this case. Whitney explained that some fifty years to the day on October 31, 1976 an older lady checked into the Parco Inn by herself. She signed in as Mrs. Martha Washington and requested room 211. After she entered her room she was not seen again until the next morning when the cleaning lady, Mrs. Missi Black went into the room to clean the room. There hanging from the ceiling was a woman dressed in a beautiful gown. The only thing that was odd about her dress was that she was missing a slipper which no one could find in the room. The coroner, Corey Pottratz, arrived and said she had hung herself around 2:11 a.m. or so. Officer Larry Robbins interviewed all the guests that night at the Parco Inn. Two motorcycle riders had spent the night at the Parco Inn and related to Officer Robbins what they thought were strange events. Their names were Jon "Evil Knievel" Lindquist and Eric "Awful" Kanawful. They said they were wakened by a strong wind that rattled their windows. Then they heard a dog bark and then a muffled noise. They both went out into the hallway of the third floor where they were staying. Directly under them they heard laughter and music. They thought the noise came from what sounded like a party in one of the rooms beneath them and thus returned to their rooms. The only other strange thing that happened that night was the town drunk, Cody Burton, stopped to get a drink at the Parco Inn and said he saw the buffalo's eyes turn red. This did not alarm anyone because Cody had on many occasions reported to the police that he had seen space ships, Martians, the Rockies winning a baseball game, and that he had talked to real live green dinosaurs in town.

Aiuto then asked, "Mrs. Anderson, do you think Mrs. Temporal killed her daughter?" Once again, Mrs. Anderson cautiously said, "We don't know, like I said, it is one of the mysteries of the Parco Inn."

Tiffany, who was very quiet as she heard the story of little Sarah; asked Mrs. Anderson, "Are there any ghosts in the Parco Inn?" Laura then said, "I believe in ghosts!" Dino Rex Hendrix then dryly joked, "Good, then you will like Casper, Wyoming!" Mrs. Hibbard was not so sure if her group from Florida needed to hear any more stories and was trying to change the subject to something more edifying when Whitney said, "there is one more story that you need to hear, the mystery of Room 218." Dino Rex Hendricks then explained that Room 218 was the only room in the Parco Inn that they could not open. It remains closed even to this day. The hinges are on the inside of the door and there is no key that works. It appears that the door is nailed shut from the inside and may even have bars securing it. All the teen-age boys and girls of the Baptist Youth Staff, including Reed, Evan and Anthony will not go near this room. Ashleigh once found little Blake Holmes wandering near Room 218 and immediately returned little Blake to his mother Sandy. The only person who has stated they were not afraid of going in to Room 218 was Margaret Tutton. However, her husband Tim said, "You wouldn't catch me dead near that room." One reason is that it is believed that this section of the Parco Inn is built over an ancient Indian burial ground. Nearby Rawlins Middle School was also built over an ancient Indian burial ground.

Room 218 has a very strange history going back to the Blizzard of 1949. The storm began on a Sunday, January 3rd. The snow continued for 35 ½ straight hours. The temperature dropped below zero. The winds then began to gust at hurricane force causing enormous snow drifts. Such drifts stopped the trains. Seventeen west-bound and seventeen east-bound trains came to a halt in front of the towns of Parco and Rawlins. Over the next month Wyoming was pasted with one blizzard after another. The Pony Express train had stopped in Rawlins. Livestock was starving in all parts of Carbon County. Phone calls were limited to three minutes. The 20-foot drifts blocked the streets and people were stranded for miles.

The Parco Inn loved snowstorms and had hosted many ski parties. Now the Parco Inn opened up her doors to all in need. Transients in fear of freezing in the stalled boxcars worked their way to the Parco Inn to sleep in its drafty halls. One of the hobos was a man by the name of Andrew "Cold-foot" Shingles. His girl friend was with him, Dorothy "Dolly" Haddone. They were wearing filthy rags and were suffering from frostbite. The electricity had gone out in half of the Parco Inn and consequently the western side of the building was pitch-black. The Parco Inn manager, Duane Comfort, said that the hobos could stay in the hallway on that side of the building to get warm, but that they really could not afford to feed them and they would be on their own for food.

In addition to several hobos who came out of the woodwork to "enjoy" the benefits of the Parco Inn, some notorious criminals came out of hiding to find lodging and food at the Parco Inn. Two such gangsters were Black Jack Ketchup and Big Nose George Parrott. They had holed up for a while at Devil's Gate but now needed the shelter of the Parco Inn. They signed their names on the register on Friday, January 13th, 1949 as Jack Mustard and George Canary. Everyone was looking at Big Nose George, because his nose was red and looked like a ski slope at Steamboat Springs. The manager felt very uncomfortable about these two shady looking characters. In fact, Duane's wife Char thought she had seen George Canary's picture at the post office for robbing a train and for killing two deputies, Fife and Taylor and for scalping a Yurka Indian. Duane gave them room 218.

In addition to hobos and gangsters there were three escaped convicts from the Rawlins State Prison who had cut through their bars with toothpaste and a piece of thread. They were now able to climb over the fence because of the 40 foot snow drift that served as a bridge for their escape. These men were likewise very hungry after surviving on prison food for several years. They were able to steal clothing from the engineers whose trains were abandoned on the tracks. The names of the three escaped convicts were Ben "the Boo" Clarence, Stephen "Hacksaw" King and Alfred "Yum-yum" Packer. They too came to find comfort at the Parco Inn. They signed the register as Benjamin Elway, James Tecumseh Hillary and William X. R. Johnsen IV, occupation: mulch men.

Needless to say, the Parco Inn was on overload with their many guests, wanted and unwanted. The blizzard continued to bring more snow and more snow and the winds averaged 60 mph for weeks. Four weeks into the blizzard, the Parco Inn ran out of food. The power lines were down and the phone lines were inoperable. The guests gathered in the lobby in front of the fireplace to stay warm. The Inn also had run out of firewood and was now using furniture and wood from the bowling alley as needed fuel to stay warm. The temperature was strikingly cold with temperatures remaining below zero for weeks. The 60 mph wind spared no one and could easily bowl over the strongest of men. Things were looking desperate and tempers began to flare. Big Nose George Parrott was looking for food with Ketchup, but found only one jack rabbit. The irony was that the Parco Inn was famous for its Jack Rabbit hunt and dinner/dance. In normal conditions, Parco was known as the best jack rabbit and jackalope territory in the west. It was not uncommon on the annual Jack Rabbit Hunt day to see the locals shoot over 50,000 rabbits and 10,000 jackalopes.

With things getting desperate and stomachs growling a strange thing began to happen. People began to disappear who were sleeping in the hallways on the west side of the second floor. First the hobos disappeared, then two of the three escaped convicts, then a couple from Hamburg, Germany, the Olsens. During this time, oddly Big Nose George and Black Jack Ketchup seemed to be quite content despite their early bellyaching regarding the food at the Parco Inn or the lack thereof. They also had grown close to convict Alfred "Yum-yum" Packer. Despite their outwardly changed attitudes towards the people, one rather rotund man from Bologna, Illinois, refused their invitation to come to room 218 when asked if he would like to come to the room for dinner.

Finally, after five weeks of blizzard-like conditions, a Chinook wind crossed the range and began to melt the snow. Aided by the persistence of road crews the roads were plowed so that food and supplies could be brought into Parco. As soon as this break in the conditions took place, Big Nose George and Black Jack Ketchup mysteriously disappeared. They did not check out of the Inn, nor did they leave their room unlocked. Joe Taylor, the aging desk clerk, said they took with them all the keys to room 218. The rest of the guests except the couple from Hamburg, checked out on the first day that the roads were clear. A. J. S., the sweetest assistant manager the Parco Inn ever had, went to see if the Olsens had left anything. She found in the Olsen's room all their clothes, Rebecca's pocketbook with money in it, empty ketchup packets, and the keys to their Studebaker which was still parked outside. This was a real mystery! Where were the Olsens from Hamburg? As the Chinook winds carved away at the snow it was reported to the manager there were bones being found in the snow on the west side of the building. Coyotes and dogs had feasted on the pile of bones, especially the Parco Inn's mascot, O. D., a red healer mix. The remains were hard to piece together due to the canines' fine work. However, forensic work identified parts of six different bodies. Oddly, the skulls they found had been cut cleanly in half. Why someone went to such effort to cut their skulls in half is still not known. The only clues to this mystery and possibly others were that the detectives also found buried under the bones a petrified piece of wood that looked like a baseball bat and one deteriorated slipper made of human skin that still had the label on it, "Made in Valley Forge."

As the group listened carefully to the story, the question was asked by Christine, "Do you think Black Jack Ketchup and Big Nose George Parrott were cannibals?" Then Jon asked a more probing question, "What remains do you think will be found if Room 218 is ever opened?" The answer came quickly from Rod Anderson, "We have no plans to open the door of Room 218. That will remain another mystery of the Parco Inn. However, what we do know about Big Nose George Parrott was that he was eventually caught and punished and presumably killed, but his body strangely disappeared. Fifty years later his body and skull were found in a fifty-gallon drum. His skull was neatly cut in two. As for Black Jack Ketchup his remains were found in the 400 ton ice house outside of town next to the mayonnaise and the relish." Rod then asked, "Who do you think did such gruesome work on Big Nose George and refrigerated Black Jack Ketchup? And where do you think such a man now might live?" The whole group then replied, "That indeed is a mystery!"

HOW TO OVERCOME FEAR!

Many names are used in this story, some real, some not. Some names are deliberately used anachronistically. It is not my intention to offend any one by my lack of historicity or by the positive or negative use of a name or a play on a name.

This short story is one part historic fact, one part fiction and two parts fabrication. This is usually how our mind works when we begin to fear. We take something that might be true and then we create something that is far worse in our minds, which is not true. We then believe the creative fabrication which further feeds our fears. The Parco Inn is rich in history. It is important to separate the myths of the Inn from the realities. Some claim the house is haunted by ghosts. First, despite local historian, Shannon, there is no such thing as good or bad ghosts or even lukewarm ghosts. However, the Bible does speak of evil spirits called demons. Demons are fallen angels who chose to follow Lucifer in his rebellion against God. Lucifer is also called Satan. The Bible calls Satan "a liar" and a "murderer." It is safe to assume that Satan and demons influence men by suggesting thoughts of murder. It is not surprising then to sense evil at the scene of the crime for this is where Satan and/or his demons successfully persuaded and deceived someone to follow through on their insidious suggestions. Such evil spirits may indeed linger in such areas to maximize the benefits of the evil. These evil spirits are demons and are not the spirits of the deceased although they can impersonate them. The spirit of the unsaved sadly goes to hell at the moment of his or her death. His spirit is confined to hell and can no longer directly influence anyone on earth. Those spirits (demons) which plagued his life can continue to plague others on earth. Such spirits may indeed haunt houses and torment people.

154

Now for the good news, God is infinitely more powerful than any creature good or bad. Satan and his fallen host are defeated foes. In every encounter between Jesus Christ and a demon, or a legion of demons in the New Testament, the demons are seen cowering in His presence and obliged to obey anything that Christ says. As Satan tempted Christ, Christ stood up to each blow by quoting an applicable passage of Scripture to resist such temptations (Matthew 4). The result was that Satan could not stand up to the power of God's Word, and had to flee. God's Word is the Dragon slayer and is called the *"sword of the Spirit."* God's Word and God's Spirit are the believer's offensive and defensive weapons in the spiritual battle. It is said that *"greater is He (God) that is in you, than he (Satan) that is in the world"* (I John 4:4). The Holy Spirit is the third Person of the Trinity and He indwells the heart of the true believer. The believer is possessed by God and can never be possessed by any other. The believer belongs to God.

Rather than slavishly fearing Satan, we should love and reverently fear God. *"Perfect love casteth out fear"* (I John 4:18). *"And fear not them which kill the body, but are not able to kill the soul: but rather fear Him (God) which is able to destroy both soul and body in hell"* (Matthew 10:28). It is only God who can send a soul to hell. We should reverentially fear God for He has the ultimate authority over our soul's eternal destiny.

It is normal for the unsaved person to fear death. God has placed that fear on the dashboard of the human heart. *"And deliver them who through fear of death were all their lifetime subject to bondage"* (I Hebrews 2:15). We should fear death if we are not a Christian, because when we die we will immediately go to a Christ-less eternity. There we will suffer for our sins in a lake of fire. No wonder we fear! We intuitively know in our heart that we will be judged for our sin and that there is more to life on the other side of physical death. There is no way to remove the fear of death except to accept the free gift of eternal life offered by the Lord Jesus Christ. *"For the wages of sin is death, but the gift of God is eternal life through Jesus Christ our Lord"* (Romans 6:23). When a person realizes that Christ paid the penalty for all of his sins on the cross he is relieved and given hope. When faith grasps that Christ arose the third day and conquered His last enemy: death; and that through Christ's death and resurrection He destroyed *"him that had the power of death, that is, the devil"* (Hebrews 2:14), he rejoices. There is no room for fear in the heart when you have Christ in your heart. He is *"the life."* Such eternal life is given to the person who repents (changes) and by faith asks Christ for forgiveness and eternal life. Have you asked the Lord into your heart to be your personal Savior? If you have, you can say with the Psalmist, *"Though I walk through the valley of the shadow of death, I will fear no evil."* If you have not, *"the valley of death"* is a very dark, lonely, and scary place to walk. As our love for God grows, all other fears are dispelled. There is no room for fear in the heart that is filled with the love of God. *"For God hath not given us the spirit of fear"* (II Timothy 1:7). He has instructed that *"what time I am afraid, I will trust in thee"* (Psalm 56:3). No matter where we are, what we are facing or what time it is; we are to trust the Lord. He will remove our fears as we pray to God and trust Him. He will give to us a peace which passes all understanding when we cast our fears on Him. (Philippians 4:7). Is your life filled with fear and anxiety? Will you trust Jesus Christ as your personal Savior?

Will you continue to trust God to overcome all of your fears? God does not want His children to live in fear but in perfect peace.

If you would like to overcome your fear of death then trust Christ as your Lord and Savior. The last chapter will explain how one can become a true Christian. The Lord will give to you the assurance in your heart that you belong to Him and that He will take you to His wonderful Heaven. *"And of some have compassion, making a difference. And others save with fear, pulling them out of the fire, hating even the garment spotted by the flesh"* (Jude 22-23).

CHAPTER FOURTEEN

THE LIFE OF A TRUE SKONGAL

I grew up in a good home where it was important for each child to be christened and assigned godparents. Several weeks after my birth, I was brought to St. Matthew's, the Episcopal Church in Paoli, Pennsylvania, where the religious leader of that church sprinkled some "holy" water on my head. At that point, the bishop pronounced to all present that I was a child of God, being baptized into the body of Christ, in the name of the Father, Son, and Holy Spirit. My parents received a certificate with this message embodied in the text. I still have this certificate on file, which certifies my becoming a "Christian" on that day. This step of faith on my parents' part was in compliance with what they had been taught by their church. I obviously cannot remember this "spiritually" significant day when I allegedly became a "Christian." At this point, the authority for my parents' actions was their church, its tradition, and its pastor. I have no doubt that their actions were sincere efforts to please God and to start me on the right road as their first born son. Of course, as a newborn babe, I had no knowledge of God, nor did I see my need for a Savior. Consequently, there was no personal, volitional relationship established between God and me at that time.

During my childhood, I vaguely remember going to church and coloring pictures of Jesus in the nursery. My knowledge of God was now being expanded. I was being taught that there was a God: one God. I was introduced to a black book, with very small print, which had no pictures. My mother also taught me the Lord's Prayer by the side of my bed and the importance of saying one's prayers at night. We also had a children's Bible with pictures in it. I remember looking through this book and can still see the page with Noah's ark. Later, when I was able to read, I read the children's Bible all the way up to the ark story and then put it aside.

When our family moved from West Chester to a country farmette in Downingtown, we stopped attending church, except for weddings, funerals, and an occasional special holiday service. My parents were disenchanted with their church and the church's apparent interest in collecting absent tithes. On at least one occasion their former church wrote to remind them that they were behind on their tithes and encouraged them to submit them as soon as possible. My parents did not like such a payment plan and made it clear to our family that this was one of the reasons we stopped going to church. I remember seeing the unused tithe envelope boxes around the house; they were the last traces of regular church attendance in our home.

Our family greatly enjoyed our small farm and country living. The only religious interruptions were the occasional visits of two men or two women who came to talk about religion. Often, my parents would hide when they saw these pairs come, or they would have one of us three boys run interference for them. By giving the uninvited visitors a dime for their literature, we could usually get rid of them. My parents did not like such confrontations with religion. Generally, we would throw out their *Watchtower* magazine and dismiss such visits as rude and untimely. I would read some of their literature, but found it totally uninteresting.

My next religious encounter was in seventh grade. We had to read a book for our literature class that dealt with a family's concern for their father to be baptized. The family was very concerned that their father would go to limbo, hell, or purgatory. Although, I don't believe such words were used, they were implied. At this point, I wondered if I would go to purgatory or hell because I was not baptized in the church on the seven hills. This thought greatly troubled me. I did not want to miss going to heaven, even though it appeared from the funerals I attended that everybody who died went to heaven regardless of how they lived on earth. It was extremely difficult for me to determine the criteria for going to heaven. It appeared that keeping some of the Ten Commandments and being sincere about what you believe was what was important. However, the book we read in class bothered me because baptism seemed to be the key that opened the door to heaven.

Because many of my friends were Catholic, I asked my mother what the difference was between an Episcopalian and a Catholic. She said Episcopalians were Protestants that had broken off from the Catholic Church. To me it appeared that the Episcopalians were Junior Varsity Catholics who were simply too lazy to learn the Latin. Regardless, I now knew I was a Protestant, but what differences or points of Catholic doctrine was I protesting? I envied my Catholic friends because it appeared they were in the superior church and maybe held the key to heaven. Several of my friends actually liked going to their Catholic Church, which led me to attend several Catholic masses. I also remember attending several Catholic weddings where everyone at the reception seemed to hit the booze pretty hard, even the priests. These actions were somewhat confusing to me as a young lad, but apparently it was okay to drink as a Catholic as long as it was not in church.

The summer after eighth grade I was invited to attend my first and only Vacation Bible School at an American Baptist church in Eagle, Pennsylvania. The pastor's daughter, Debbie Heggarty, a classmate of mine, invited me. I was always impressed with Debbie. Although not the prettiest or the most popular girl in our class, she was respected. She had a wholesome air about her. She was a straight-A student, an aggressive athlete, and the leader of the field hockey and basketball teams. I can still see her making a half-court shot at the buzzer to win the game for the Lionville Lions. She also dressed differently than the others in our public school. At this time it was still illegal for the girls to wear pants to school, so they all had to wear dresses. Debbie's dresses were knee-length, whereas most of the other girls were belt-length.

When she invited me to VBS in June of 1971 I had nothing else to do and was bored silly at home, so I said, "Yes." Vacation Bible School sounded somewhat childish and beneath me, but Debbie said the older kids would play basketball each day as well. My mother agreed to take me to the Baptist church each day, some 5 miles from home and near to where she grew up. In fact, she had attended this church on occasion as a young girl. However, she was somewhat turned off by their beliefs and by the duplicity of some of the people in the church. I asked her what the difference was between an Episcopalian and a Baptist. It appeared that there were some differences, one being that the Baptists were historically farmers and uneducated; their services were not as formal as even the low-church of the Episcopal denomination, and they were Bible-thumpers who preached hell fire and brimstone. (Later, I assured my mom that I would never be a Baptist.)

Once at the VBS, I realized that I was probably the "oldest" in the midst of some fifty or so little rug rats. This made me feel a little uncomfortable, but Debbie did all she could to make me feel welcomed. I think she may have liked me, but I am not sure, because attending the VBS was Linda Hagerstrom. That week I concentrated on impressing Linda and hardly gave Debbie the time of day. I don't remember much from the VBS, other than the craft I made, a note pad holder, which I kept for years. However, on the second to last day of VBS, while listening to a Bible lesson in a garage across from the church, I responded. The teacher asked, "If you would die today and believe you would go to heaven, raise your hand." I could not raise my sweaty hand because I was not sure. He then asked, "If you could not raise your hand to that question, but would like to know, then raise your hand." I think there were only six or so in our class. I cheated and watched everyone raise their hands to the first question and almost simultaneously raised my hand with Linda Hagerstrom at the second question. Linda and I were the only two who responded to the Gospel that day. My motives for raising my hand were probably mixed at that time.

The teacher then said to Linda and me that he wanted to take us over to the parsonage for the pastor to talk to us about how to get saved. It had been pouring all day, so the three of us ran quickly to the large house. While waiting for the pastor to come home, I enjoyed the freshly baked chocolate chip cookies that Mrs. Heggarty had made and played Nerf basketball in the kitchen. Mrs. Heggarty was a very pleasant person and seemed to be very happy.

Finally, Pastor Heggarty came in; he took off his hat and his rubber boots. He looked terrible. He had just returned from a funeral which he had conducted in the downpour and was drenched. He probably was hungry and cold and was looking forward to a quiet uninterrupted lunch; however, before him were two young people looking for the answer to the most important question in life: "how do you get to heaven?"

The pastor took us both back to his study and opened up his black Bible, which had many verses underlined and notes written in it. It almost looked like he regularly read the Bible, which was a very foreign concept to me. I thought this especially strange since every church Bible I had seen before looked brand new sitting on a reading stand. Regardless, he opened the Bible and explained verses from a book called Romans. At the end of his talk, he asked if we would like to call upon the name of the Lord to forgive us and to save us from our sins. We both jumped at such an opportunity. He led us in what he called a sinner's prayer, which I was not familiar with but readily prayed. After praying, I sensed a peace flood my soul that I had never experienced before. I was so happy! I could not wait to tell my mom what happened.

When my mom did come to pick me up, she anxiously started our conversation by telling me that the basement of our house was flooding and that our neighbor's basement and backyard were under water too. It had been raining now for almost two weeks, and the Brandywine River was ready to crest its banks. She was very worried. In fact, one may recall Hurricane Cruella Deville and the terrible flood in eastern Pennsylvania in 1971.

While mom explained the flood conditions, I felt that maybe later I would tell her about the joy I had just experienced as I knew my sins were forgiven. I will never forget that day. Sadly, the next day I returned to my old sinful habits of beating up my brothers, listening to the music of a pastor's son who changed his name to Alice, looking at ungodly magazines, etc. I did not know how to get the joy back and maintain it. For the next eight years I would continue to fall deeper into the miry clay.

The next day, I would not be able to return to VBS because of the storm and water problems. Several weeks after the floods of joy experience of VBS, Debbie Heggarty invited me to Sunday school and to the morning church service. My mother agreed to drop me off and to pick me up later. I thought it strange that she would not join me at church, but she had a lot to do at home and did not feel comfortable with some of the people in the church. In Sunday school, we were given a study guide and had a Bible lesson. I hoped and prayed the teacher would not ask me any religious questions or ask me to find and read a passage in the Bible. Everyone in the class seemed to be very familiar with the Bible, which made me feel increasingly uncomfortable.

I can still remember a part of the sermon when Pastor Heggarty told the congregation how he was converted from a wicked life in a motorcycle gang. It greatly impressed me that a gang member was now a straight-laced preacher. It was almost too hard to believe. It was hard for me to envision mild-mannered Pastor Heggarty on a motorcycle, getting drunk, and fighting with chains.

I was so excited about church that the next week I took my bad-news friend, Slow Joe, to church with me. My mom joked about the two choirboys. That morning in the church service, Joe made all kinds of funny faces and noises to distract me and to get me to laugh in the service. He did a very good job. After church, when we were back at home, he persuaded me that going to church was really a waste of time and that the next Sunday we needed to go fishing or swimming. I weakly agreed and ceased going to church.

Two years later, Joe and I attended a church service with his mother. It was a United Methodist church. I asked my mother what the difference was between the

Episcopal Church and the Methodist Church. It appeared that there were not too many differences and that there were not too many absolutes anyone could know. I assumed once again that it was not the object of your faith that really mattered, but that your faith be sincere. One absolute I was learning was that all churches were filled with hypocrites. This church was no exception.

It was hard to listen to the pastor for several reasons. One, Joe was making his funny faces and sounds to get me to laugh, which he did successfully not only with me, but with all of the kids near to us. Secondly, the pastor's son had been expelled that year from our school for blowing up a commode. Once he returned to school, our bandleader asked Jeff to explain to the class how he made the bomb. It was music to Jeff's ears to present to the class his devious creation. During the church service, it was hard to reconcile the pastor's message on love with his son's drug problems and his love for destruction.

Once in high school, I can only remember two confrontations with religion. One was attending a Young Life meeting, or a meeting something like that at Heidi Parvin's house. They said it was a Christian youth meeting. All I recall is the guys and girls kissing and talking about trying to get some beer.

The other experience was much more convicting. It was in eleventh grade. Slow Joe and I were on the bus going to school. We were both sitting in the back. Slow Joe then had the bright idea to skip school that day. The plan was simple. When the bus arrived at school we would duck behind the back seat until everyone got off, then we would continue to hide without laughing until the bus driver would park the bus and then we would sneak out and escape.

Again, I yielded to temptation, while everyone else got off the bus in front of Downingtown High School we hid. My heart was racing as I listened to the bus pull away. We both wondered if anybody ratted on us, or if he knew we had not gotten off the bus. We listened to him shift through the gears until he was moving at a steady rate on a major highway. We correctly guessed, we were on Route 30, but once he got off we had no idea where he was taking us.

After what seemed like hours, the bus came to a stop, and was turned off. We heard the door being shut and locked. We waited and waited and finally looked up. When I looked up, the first thing I saw was a cross. I did not know this, but our driver was a pastor of a church. He had parked at the church and gone inside. Tremendous conviction of sin pierced my heart. Sadly, such conviction was quickly set aside as Joe and I jumped out of the bus and ran for cover. My heart was empty as we walked the five or so miles home, trying not to be seen by friend or foe.

During my high school years, I drifted further and further from the cross of Christ. I began to get involved in alcohol and drugs. Sports were still a part of my life, but that interest was being replaced with motorcycles. I began to race motocross and spent much of my time partying and looking in the rear view mirror. I was intrigued with bikers and with their "clubs." I knew I could ride with the best of them, and with my shoulder-length hair, I fit right in. But I had a terrible fear of guns, fighting, chains, and boas. This all disqualified me from being a Warlock. During this same time period, my parents were having marital problems, which lead ultimately to their divorce in my junior year. I used their divorce as an excuse to further my rebellion and seek attention. After shattering a windshield with a BB gun, Slow Joe and I ran away to Florida. This nightmare and other incidents created an environment where the police were routinely visiting or driving by my house. The life I was living was anything but Christian! There was no evidence of genuine salvation, except for a conscience that seemed to work overtime.

My mother remarried and we moved during my senior year. I began to attend Twin Valley High School near Reading, Pennsylvania. I had determined that I would try to get back in sports and make the best out of this fresh start. I was not seeking to reform, but only to reload. I actually started to jog again to get in shape for basketball and thought it would be best not to smoke dope. I even got a haircut before we moved so one could almost see my ears.

During my senior year my only religious encounter was with the girl I dated who was a Catholic. I attended one or two church services with her and her family. The family did not like that I was not a Catholic. Her parents were very active in their Catholic Church. They also had some reservations about my taking her to the prom and other activities. For this and other reasons, Matilda and I chose to run away together. Once again I found myself in Florida running from parents, the law, and my conscience.

Needless to say, when we returned several days later her parents were not happy with me. The first thing they did was take her to church and confession with the priest. I thought her father, an ex-Marine, would kill me. Fortunately, he had enough religion simply to forbid me from seeing his daughter again.

The summer after I graduated from high school, I began my third summer of employment at a hearse company. It was my job to wash, wax, and deliver the hearses, ambulances and school buses for Wolfington's. The hearses intrigued me especially and were used in a handful of memorable pranks. In wood shop my senior year, I built a coffin for my senior project. I had hoped to use it on prom night in the back of a borrowed hearse, but for some reason Matilda was not so merry about the idea. Now with no Maltilda, no plans for college, and few friends, I was very discouraged. The daily work on the hearses was a nagging reminder of death and that the day would come when I would ride in the back. I was dying within; the void was enormous. Daily my emptiness was being magnified. I had to do something. That fall, I quit my job at the hearse company when my boss was fired. I looked for a more challenging job, which I found pumping gas at two gas stations.

During the fall of 1976, I had two more religious encounters. The first one was while I was shooting baskets at a park in Elverson. There was a girl there who had attended a nearby Christian high school, High Point Baptist Academy, and a college called Bob Jones University. I had never heard of Bob Jones University. The girl was friendly and wholesome, but somewhat apprehensive about talking with a heathen. She talked about how much she loved her college. I was somewhat apprehensive too, because I thought maybe her school was founded by some guy who did the Kool Aid thing in Guyana or Georgia. I also asked her if she played golf. She thought that was a strange question. Looking back it appeared she wanted to say more about her being a Christian but was a little timid.

The other experience was playing basketball with a new friend, Mel Skiles, a school teacher. Mel saw a young man in need of some mentoring and took me under his wing. He had watched me play basketball at Twin Valley High School and knew that I pitched and had helped our baseball team go to the regional playoffs. Mel included me on his baseball team (sponsored by a beer distributor); a semi-pro, fast-pitch softball team (sponsored by the Elverson Hotel and Bar); and his basketball team (sponsored by the Country Tavern).

While at a practice, Mel introduced me to a Lutheran pastor who was working out with them. When I met the pastor, I thought it was really cool that a minister could play basketball and did not always have to wear robes. He even played and talked like the rest of our team. I so wished that he would invite me to his church, but he did not. I actually drove to his church and waited in the parking lot, hoping for a providential meeting with the pastor. Unfortunately, all I saw were tombstones in the church's cemetery and again death fears were knocking on the door.

It did not take me long working at the Amoco and Hess stations to realize that this was not what I wanted to do for the rest of my life, so I applied to several colleges. Before I got involved in partying in high school, I was pretty much a straight-A student. Even with the partying, I was a B student, so my grades were high enough to get into most colleges.

I applied to Wilson College and was rejected because it was an all-girl's school. I then considered going to a college called Brigham Young because I liked the name. I did not know that it was a Mormon school. Then I applied to Elizabethtown College at the recommendation of my high school baseball coach. He had attended there and knew the baseball coach well. He thought that I could get a partial baseball scholarship. I applied and was quickly accepted for the spring semester of 1977.

On Super Bowl Sunday, in a snowstorm, I moved into the third floor of Ober dormitory. I was excited about the prospects of a new start and even got a haircut the day before; now one could see half of my ears. I purposed in my heart to study hard, not to party, and to make the baseball team. That semester only one of my three goals was met. I won my first baseball game against Ursinus College and by the end of the season had the most wins on the pitching staff.

During the semester, I encountered several campus ministries. I actually went on a hayride with one group. It was very boring until the leader lost his wallet in the hay. It was then amusing to watch how angry he got and how anxious he was to find it. Needless to say, his testimony did not shine through.

On another occasion I attended a meeting where all we did was sit in a circle and sing *Cum Ba Ya* five hundred times as we stared at a candle. Everyone was to testify as to what he or she saw. I said I saw a candle and then walked out into the dark. During that semester I attended church one time on Palm Sunday (Church of the Brethren, the campus church).

On that Sunday each person received a palm branch. I had no idea of its significance but thought it was pretty neat to carry it to the campus cafeteria after the service. I really thought I was pious and even looked down at others for not attending such a meaningful service and missing out on receiving their palm branch. These thoughts were indeed the height of hypocrisy, because I strolled into the cafeteria with the girl that I had partied and danced with the night before. We both held our palm leaves in the same manner that Adam and Eve wore their fig leaves. On another occasion, I attended a service for Catholics on campus and received ashes on my forehead. I had no idea of the meaning, but I felt really good inside and felt that I had made up some lost ground with God. That year I was truly an A & P Christian: Ashes and Palms.

My sophomore year was darker than my freshman year. I now was fully engrossed in a life of licentiousness. I was now mocking God, Christianity, and religion. As a joke, I changed my major from psychology to religion. I joked that I read my Bible and regularly attended St. Mattress above Holy Springs Church. I even applied and received an ordination certificate from a Universalist church in California which I proudly displayed in the local bars.

During this year I received the nickname "Sick Will." Sadly, I lived up to that name. Despite my highly inflated view of myself and outward success in baseball (I ended the season with the second highest statistics in the nation in Division III baseball and the prospects of being drafted after my junior year.) I was still very empty. I exchanged peace and joy for further confusion and guilt.

During the summer I worked with my uncle in his landscaping business. We would regularly conclude our day of work at a local gin mill or having a Blue Ribbon at his house. I enjoyed the sense of family and admired my uncle's ability to enjoy life. He treated me like a son. Sadly, several years later he tried to take his life illustrating that something was missing. I also played some baseball sponsored by a beer distributor, but spent most of my spare time partying and getting in trouble.

That summer I spent one night in jail in New Jersey. I was innocent of the crime that I was accused of but felt no injustice, because I had committed other crimes and gotten away with them. Fortunately, I was vindicated and released. Unfortunately, it had very little effect on me. There is no question in my mind that apart from the grace of God, I was on a collision course with death or the state penitentiary.

My junior year was disastrous. My grades were slipping; my drinking was becoming a daily practice; and to top it off I separated my shoulder playing football; which would set me back considerably for baseball. My frustration level was increasing and so was my foolishness.

During this time, a petition was being signed to present to student government to have me expelled from Elizabethtown College for my rowdy behavior. At the appointed meeting, my baseball coach and some of the team stood up for me and persuaded the board and those on student government to give me another chance. I told them that I would turn over a new leaf. I could have turned over the whole tree, but there still was no true change in my heart. However, since my crimes did not involve murder, the board agreed to give me one more chance.

During the spring semester I had two classes called "Religion in America" and "New Testament Survey." In these classes, I was bored to death as Dr. "Snatch-your-soul" pontificated on his views of religion and the Bible. Although never clearly illustrated, we were instructed that the Bible was filled with errors. We learned of the mysterious and missing Q-source and of letters like JEDP that we needed to know for our exam. Some of the students would challenge the teacher on what they said were liberal views on the Bible. I thought they were disrespectful and wished that they would just shut up. I remember asking Dr. "Snatch-your-soul" one question in class, "What does it mean to be a Good Samaritan?" He did not know where it was in the Bible, but he did explain the story to me. I tried to fight back tears as he related the story of the one who went out of his way and sacrificed for someone in need, suggesting that Jesus was a Good Samaritan. I was convicted right there in class by the moral purity and integrity of the Good Samaritan.

During this time, I met a new friend; his name was Jim. Jim was unlike most students; he was highly disciplined. Jim woke up at 6:00 a.m. each morning, worked out and studied hard. He partied hard, but it appeared that he was feeling increasingly uncomfortable with such a lifestyle. During the summers, Jim had been selling books for the Southwestern Book Company and had made a heap of money. Jim began to talk to me about working with him that summer and selling books. He gave me books and tapes on selling; Zig Ziglar was his hero. Jim was also establishing the habit of reading the Bible. I had never read or owned a Bible but strangely had been given two Bibles that year at Christmas, one from my Uncle Jim Cooke and one from my grandmother Chips.

Jim's example led me to take my Bible with me when our baseball team went to spring training in Florida. I had no intentions of reading the Bible in Florida, but the way my year was going, I thought I needed every advantage I could get, and if carrying a Bible would help, then so be it. Oddly, waking up in Florida with a nasty bender (not a breaking pitch) and missing the team bus to the practice field, I found myself all alone in the dorms. Feeling guilty, I opened the Bible in my bag and began to read it. It comforted my heart. I then put it back in my bag and hitched a ride to practice with some girl I met in the cafeteria.

Jim continued aggressively to persuade me to sell books that summer. I would have liked to have had the opportunity to play in a league like the Cape Cod league, but had a very mediocre season and was not given any invitations. I had tried out for the Philadelphia Phillies the summer before and would be scouted by the Phillies and several other teams, but for some reason unknown to me, nothing was panning out. By default, and Jim's persistence, I found myself in sales school with Jim in Nashville, Tennessee. Jim was a workhorse. He tricked me: sales school was hard work. I hated hard work. I also had no car, and now saw why Jim wanted me to ride with him. I was trapped. I could not easily get to the bars, and soon we would be given a location far from home. During the two weeks of sales school, I did not get drunk. This was a record. I began to think clearly and noticed the birds singing. I stopped for a moment to smell the roses. I then began to ask myself, "Where have I been, what am I doing, and where am I going?" I did not like my sobriety because it was forcing me to face life and reality.

After sales school, Jim's team was assigned to work in Sedalia, Missouri. We left school singing over and over "We are family" and headed west. Jim permitted me to have two beers since I had been a good boy at sales school. We arrived Saturday night at our destination and three of us moved into a basement apartment. I had to share a bed with one of the other guys. We only had one car, but it was tempting to saddle up the cockroaches in the basement and ride them to town. Jim decided that we should all go to church the next day and then begin selling our books on Monday. We agreed. On Sunday we went to a Nazarene church. The pastor preached on a story from the Bible that I had never heard before: the Prodigal Son. He even mentioned in his sermon that there might be some young man in the service that day who was far from home and far from God. I thought Jim had told the preacher all about me. I was very uncomfortable with the message, especially when the preacher said that the Prodigal Son had to come to himself and hit rock bottom before he could come home to God. During the next two weeks that message would haunt me. I was definitely living in a pigpen and also felt like I had spent all my substance. In fact, I now had no money and asked Jim for a loan. He agreed thinking it would be additional motivation for me to sell those books.

During the next two weeks, I was in total despair. Missouri would show me I needed to be broken of all self-dependence. I was being stretched beyond measure. I hated my job. Not intentionally, but I was given the poorest section of Sedalia. The last thing most of the people needed were dictionaries. This would serve as my excuse for not working hard and for not selling the books. As I walked through town, I saw a church with a high steeple. I walked to its steps and sat down. It was there that I prayed to a God that I did not know, "God, if you are real, please help me. If you would help me get back to Pennsylvania, I will be a better person. Amen."

I knew Jim would not be happy with my quitting and would persuade me to stay, so I thought just to leave him a note would suffice. After packing my three large bags, I began my journey, hitchhiking back to Pennsylvania with the resolve to be a better person. The journey began at the exit for Sedalia, Missouri on I-70. This reformation lasted only to my first ride, when I yielded to a Coors beer and a joint. After the driver dropped me off in St. Louis, I had a difficult time finding a ride and began to ask truck drivers to assist me. To motivate them I told them my car had broken down and that I needed to get home to Pennsylvania for my wedding. The truck drivers were a great blessing to me and did all they could to get me to "my wedding" on time. They would call ahead on their CB and arrange each ride for me on the routes I needed to go. I could not have gotten home faster if I had driven myself. I also made more money from the truck drivers than I did selling books as I capitalized on their goodness.

Once back in Pennsylvania, I stayed briefly with my friend Rick in Harrisburg and then went back to my college to talk with my baseball coach about the possibility of my living with him for the summer. He was glad to see me and was looking for someone to housesit for the summer. Being the responsible person I was, he turned his house over to me: brave man. The stipulations were no partying in the house and that the hot-water heater would be turned off for the summer. I agreed. All I needed now was a job, which was quickly granted to me after calling Gay Graham's father, who owned a nuts and bolt factory in Lancaster. I still did not have any transportation but that did not hinder me from getting to work each day. I had a golden thumb and enjoyed hitchhiking the 20 miles to work and meeting new people.

Two rides that summer were extremely memorable. The first was when a VW bus pulled over to pick me up. Inside the van was a Mennonite woman wearing her plain clothes and prayer cap. I knew right away that this would be a safe ride. Not all of my rides were the safe kind; the problem was she did not know if her passenger was safe. She asked me where I was going and then went on to tell me that she never had picked up a hitchhiker in her life. She also mentioned that her husband would kill her if he knew what she was doing, but she said that today when she saw me that God had told her to pick me up. I looked around the van and wondered how God gave her such information. She went on to tell me how good God was. I was very happy for her but also happy to get out. After arriving at the nuts and bolts factory, I was reminded again that my life was messed up. Every day I weighed the nuts, or screws, or bolts and put the oily items into packaging boxes and got them ready to be picked up by UPS or our delivery truck. The daily message was loud and clear: I was nuts and my life was a little screwy to say the least.

The second memorable ride was with a man who was a former alcoholic who said he was now "born again." I did not know what this meant, other than a political label that was criticized around our dinner table. He told me his story of getting "saved." I was not sure what he meant by being "saved." I assumed "saved" from a life of alcohol. He went on to tell me that he repented of his sins: sins that had paralleled those in my life. He went on to tell me how he had asked Jesus Christ to be his personal Savior. He said He was fully trusting in Christ for "salvation."

He then went on to tell me about his three brothers and how he had tried to persuade them to be "born again." His first brother, he related, laughed at him and said that he was too young to think about religion. Tragically, shortly after this, his brother fell into the lake, while drinking and fishing, and drowned. Then he related to me how he had "witnessed" to his second brother. Likewise, this brother rejected his message and said he might consider God later, but was having too much fun right now. Tragically, shortly after talking to his second brother, his unsaved brother was killed at work by a swinging I-beam. Finally, he tried to "save" his last surviving brother. This brother did not want to hear about religion and rejected the offer to be "born again." Unbelievably, shortly after "witnessing" to this brother, his brother arrived home drunk, pulled into his garage, fell asleep in the car while leaving the engine running, and died because of the fumes.

I wondered why he was sharing these horror stories with me, but then it became obvious. He wanted me to be "born again." After he asked me if I was "saved," I confidently said yes that I was a Christian. He then dropped me off under the bridge on Route 383 near Elizabethtown. I walked from there to the farmhouse knowing that I had lied to the man. I didn't know if I was "saved." I was not 100 percent sure that if I died I would go to heaven. To be safe, for awhile I stayed away from garages, I-beams, and fishing trips. I was glad when this summer was over, despite having a new girl friend, and playing baseball for the East Shore League.

During the summer I had become friends with a guy I had previously despised, Al Heney. Al was a big guy with a Honda motorcycle and a fumanchu mustache. He had just gotten involved in jogging and was starting to get in fabulous shape. He even gave me a pair of his running shoes in exchange for some of Coach Wright's eggs. Al had run across a world-class runner that summer, Carol Friedly, who was being trained by Arthur Lydiard. Carol and her husband had taken an interest in Al and were giving him training information. She also invited Al to a Bible study that her church was conducting at a house outside of town. Al attended the study and was very enthusiastic about it. He related to me what he had been learning and even how the Bible spoke about sports and running. I agreed to attend one of the Bible studies but made it clear that I was not interested in any commitments to it.

On a weeknight in the fall of 1979, I attended my first real Bible study. Was I ever surprised when I entered the house to see that it was a ladies' Bible study! There was one man in attendance, but he was retarded. The woman teaching the Bible study was somewhat over-weight, missing several teeth, and wearing a large hat with fruit on it. I was looking for a bird to fly out at any moment. I tried not to laugh at the scene and sat down respectfully. She was teaching on the subject of Dispensationalism. I had never heard the word, but I quickly found out that it was something that dealt with prophecy and the end times. I was enamored by the topic as well as the clear presentation given by Mrs. Luella Keener. Did she ever know the Bible! She even covered some prophecies that dealt with the second coming of Christ. The only teaching I had ever heard or seen on this subject was on the back of a stop sign on Route 113 which said, "Jesus is coming again."

After the study I returned to my basement apartment. I pulled out my Bible which I had read last in Florida during spring training. This time the Bible would never return to the shelf. I began reading in Matthew and during the next few weeks read the entire New Testament. Each time I opened the Scriptures I sensed a unique peace that I was reading a love letter from God to me. I also continued to attend the Bible study. After each study, I would stand around asking Mrs. Keener a million questions from dinosaurs to UFOs. She also clearly presented the plan of salvation: how Jesus died for my sins, was buried, and rose again so that I could be forgiven if I called upon Him in faith. Finally, in the privacy of my apartment, I cried out to God in faith and said, "Dear Lord, be merciful to me a sinner. I believe you died on the cross for my sins. Lord, I don't want to play any games with my soul. I may have been saved at VBS, but if not, then please save me now; I need Your forgiveness. Please come in to my heart and be my personal Savior and help me live for You through Your power. I pray in Jesus name, Amen."

Whether I was saved at VBS or on that night in 1979, only the Lord knows, but I do know now that I am a child of God because of His grace. I am so thankful for His forgiveness and His free gift of eternal life. My hope and assurance are in the Lord and not in any of my good works. I am trusting Christ's atoning death for my salvation, and as Jesus rose from the grave, I believe that I will rise on the resurrection morning with a body like His. If asked today if I would go to heaven, I can say with full assurance, "Yes, because of the grace of God." After trusting Christ as my personal Savior, I began attending Mt. Calvary Bible Church of Elizabethtown, Pennsylvania. It was there that I was taught the fundamentals of the Faith: that there are spiritual absolutes; that faith must have an object, Jesus Christ, and that the Bible teaches that you can *"know that ye have eternal life"* (I John 5:13).

I have shared with you my spiritual journey. I am eternally grateful to be a Christian. I would love to hear from you to hear where you are spiritually. Are you searching? Are you a born-again Christian? Do you know, with 100 percent certainty, that when you die you will go to heaven? If not, would you call out in faith to the Lord Jesus to save you? Would you like to know further how you can be 100 percent sure that you are going to heaven?

To be saved you must:

1) Repent (turn from your sins) and confess to God that you are a sinner. Not only are we a sinner (Romans 3:23), but the *"wages of sin"* is eternal separation from God (Romans 6:23). God would be perfectly just to condemn any sinner to hell.

2) Believe that Jesus Christ, the Son of God, left heaven above to come to this earth to die for your sins on the cross. Jesus was your substitute Who paid your sin debt by shedding His blood on the cross (I Peter 3:18). We are saved by the atoning work of Christ. He cried from the cross, *"It is finished."* There is nothing we can do to add to the finished work of Christ for salvation. Jesus Christ did all the work.

3) Believe in your heart that God raised His Son from the dead on the third day following Christ's crucifixion (Romans 10:9). By the resurrection of Christ, we are instructed that God the Father accepted Christ's sacrifice in our behalf and that because of Him we can have victory over the grave, death and hell. We have a living Savior that wants us to fellowship and enjoy Him forever in heaven!

4) Call upon the Lord in faith for salvation and forgiveness. You must come to the point that you see that you cannot save yourself (Ephesians 2:8-9) and that you must trust/rely upon the Lord Jesus Christ alone for salvation. Salvation can only be received by asking in faith for it. Salvation is the *"gift of God."*

If you want forgiveness and salvation from death and hell, please cry out in faith to God:

Dear Lord, be merciful to me a sinner. I believe that you died for me on the cross and that you rose again. Please enter into my heart and life. Forgive me of my sins and become my personal Lord and Savior. I pray in Jesus' name.

If you have prayed to accept Christ or have any spiritual questions please feel free to write me at:

Dr. William J. Senn, III
6953 West 92nd Lane
Westminster, CO 80021
or email me at: wsenn@tricitybaptist.org

APPENDIX A: COLORADO SNOW

THE TALE END OF THE STORY - CHAPTER ONE

PSALM 51:7, "*Purge me with hyssop, and I shall be clean: wash me, and I shall be whiter than snow.*"

ISAIAH 1:18, "*Come now, and let us reason together, saith the Lord: though your sins be as scarlet, they shall be as white as snow, though they be red like crimson, they shall be as wool.*"

THE COLORADO PSALM – PSALM 121
(121:1) I will lift up mine eyes unto the hills, from whence cometh my help.
(121:2) My help cometh from the LORD, which made heaven and earth.
(121:3) He will not suffer thy foot to be moved: he that keepeth thee will not slumber.
(121:4) Behold, he that keepeth Israel shall neither slumber nor sleep.
(121:5) The LORD is thy keeper: the LORD is thy shade upon thy right hand.
(121:6) The sun shall not smite thee by day, nor the moon by night.
(121:7) The LORD shall preserve thee from all evil: he shall preserve thy soul.
(121:8) The LORD shall preserve thy going out and thy coming in from this time forth, and even for evermore.
Daily we enjoy gazing in awe at the Rocky Mountains. Long's Peak is framed by several of our windows in our house. This peak especially tantalizes me. It taunts me by saying, "I double-dog dare you to climb me!" These mountains scare me but they also encourage me. Psalm 121 I have read at every graveside funeral I have conducted in Colorado. I have affectionately called this Psalm, the Colorado Psalm.
1. By reading Psalm 121, how can you be comforted by looking up to the Rocky Mountains?
2. The Prophet Isaiah states that we can have our sins washed "*as white as snow.*" What can wash away our sin?
3. How does God forgive sin?
4. What must we do to be forgiven?

THE TALE END OF THE SERMON - CHAPTER TWO

NUMBERS 32:23, *"But if ye will not do so, behold, ye have sinned against the Lord: and be sure your sin will find you out."*

GALATIANS 6:7-8, *"Be not deceived; God is not mocked: for whatsoever a man soweth, that shall he also reap. For he that soweth to his flesh shall of the flesh reap corruption; but he that soweth to the Spirit shall of the Spirit reap life everlasting."*

1. What behaviors or activities in this story are not appropriate for a Christian? Why?
2. What should the boy, who threw the egg, have done when the bus driver stopped the school bus the first time?
3. What is the Biblical truth illustrated in what takes place in the story one year later to the day of the boy's egg toss?
4. Give a Biblical example where this principle is illustrated.
5. Have you seen this Biblical principle operative in your life in any unique ways? Please describe.
6. If you have not trusted the Lord as your Savior and had all your sins forgiven, then when will all of your sins find you out?
7. When does God ultimately itemize all of the sins of one's life and punish the sinner?

APPENDICITIS C: THE GREAT PUMPKIN RIDE

THE TALE END OF THE SERMON – CHAPTER THREE

ROMANS 3:24-25a, *"Being justified freely by his grace through the redemption that is in Christ Jesus: Whom God hath set forth to be a propitiation through faith in his blood,"*

I TIMOTHY 2:5, *"For there is one God, and one mediator between God and men, the man Christ Jesus;"*

I JOHN 2:2, *"And he [Christ] is the propitiation for our sins: and not for our's only, but also for the sins of the whole world."*
1. Why should the father be angry with his son? What things did he do wrong?
2. Who in the story helped appease the father's anger? What did he do to change the father's wrath?
3. Why is it said in the Bible that God is angry with us?
4. Can you be angry with someone and still love them?
5. What did Christ do to remove God's anger towards sinners and towards our sin?
6. Who took God's wrath for us and suffered the punishment we deserved?
7. If you have been forgiven by God, is He still angry with you?

APPENDIX D: FROSHMAN THE SNOWMAN

THE TALE END OF THE SERMON – CHAPTER FOUR

EPHESIANS 2:1 and 2:5, *"And you hath he quickened, who were dead in trespasses and sins; ... Even when we were dead in sins, hath quickened us together with Christ, [by grace ye are saved;]."*

EPHESIANS 2:8-10, *"For by grace are ye saved through faith; and that not of yourselves: it is the gift of God: Not of works, lest any man should boast. For we are his workmanship, created in Christ Jesus unto good works, which God hath before ordained that we should walk in them."*

1. Who said, "You can fool some of the people some of the time, but you can't fool all of the people all of the time?"
2. Who was fooled in this story and why?
3. There are many people today who are fooling themselves, thinking that they are Christians, but who have never been genuinely born again. What are some of Satan's ways of deceiving people to think they have spiritual life?
4. Some people give the outward appearance of being a Christian, but inwardly their heart is as cold as ice. Why do people pretend to be something they are not?
5. Could the snowman have moved? Could it come to life? What would it take for the Snowman to come to life?
6. We are taught in the Bible that we are *"dead in sins."* How are we made alive spiritually?

APPENDIX E: JONAH AND THE ENGAGEMENT RING

THE TALE END OF THE SERMON – CHAPTER FIVE

JONAH 1:2-3, *"Arise, go to Nineveh, that great city, and cry against it; for their wickedness is come up before me. But Jonah rose up to flee unto Tarshish from the presence of the Lord, and went down to Joppa; and he found a ship going to Tarshish: so he paid the fare thereof, and went down into it, to go with them unto Tarshish from the presence of the Lord."*

ACTS 13:13, *"Now when Paul and his company loosed from Paphos, they came to Perga in Pamphylia: and John departing from them returned to Jerusalem."*

1. Have you ever run from God or from spiritual responsibilities?
2. Who has kept you from making the wrong decisions in life or warned you of the dangerous path that you were traveling?
3. Can you give an example in your own life where your plans did not work out, but the Lord used the circumstances for good anyway?
4. Who has made a spiritual contribution to your life and how?
5. What was the most important thing lost in the story?

APPENDECTOMY F: THE PEACEFUL VACATION

THE TALE END OF THE SERMON – CHAPTER SIX

PROVERBS 24:10, "*If thou faint in the day of adversity, thy strength is small.*"

ISAIAH 40:29-30, "*He giveth power to the faint; and to them that have no might he increaseth strength. Even the youths shall faint and be weary, and the young men shall utterly fall: But they that wait upon the Lord shall renew their strength: they shall mount up with wings as eagles; they shall run, and not be weary; and they shall walk, and not faint.*"

LUKE 18:1, "*And he spake a parable unto them to this end, that men ought always to pray, and not to faint;*"

GALATIANS 6:9, "*And let us not be weary in well doing: for in due season we shall reap, if we faint not.*"

1. What is the major theme of this story and what is the one phrase or word that reoccurs through the entire chapter that reinforces that theme?
2. What verses come to your mind, that are not listed above, that you could use when you are going through trials?
3. What do missionaries on deputation have in common with "THE PEACEFUL VACATION"?
4. What differences are there between a missionary on deputation and a family on a stressful "vacation"?
5. How do you generally handle trials?
6. What are some wrong ways to handle trials?
7. Have you had anyone close in your family die? What verses in the Bible would you use to comfort those who have lost a loved one?

APOTHEOSIS G: TOP COPS AND A LOWLY PREACHER

THE TALE END OF THE SERMON – CHAPTER SEVEN

GENESIS 15:1, *"Fear not Abram: I am thy shield, and thy exceeding great reward."*

PSALM 28:7, *"The Lord is my strength and my shield; my heart trusted in him, and I am helped: therefore my heart greatly rejoiceth; and with my song will I praise him."*

PSALM 91:4, *"He shall cover thee with his feathers, and under his wings shalt thou trust: his truth shall be thy shield and buckler."*

PROVERBS 30:5, *"Every word of God is pure: he is a shield unto them that put their trust in him."*

1. What were the dangers involved in this story?
2. What was the most dangerous thing that you have ever faced?
3. What are your fears?
4. Can you list any close calls that you have had, where the Lord has protected you?
5. Can you recall any spiritual close calls where the Lord protected you from error, or the wrong group, cult, church, etc.? What is your best defense when you are afraid?

APPENDIX H: WINDSOR'S NIGHT IN JAIL

THE TALE END OF THE SERMON – CHAPTER ATE

PROVERBS 12:10, *"A righteous man regardeth the life of his* **beast:** *but the tender mercies of the wicked are cruel."*

ECCLESIASTES 9:4, *"For to him that is joined to all the living there is hope: for* **a living dog** *is better than a dead lion."*

REVELATION 22:14-15, *"Blessed are they that do his commandments, that they may have right to the tree of life, and may enter in through the gates into the city.* **For without are dogs,** *and sorcerers, and whoremongers, and murderers, and idolaters, and whosoever loveth and maketh a lie."*

1. Have you ever felt like no one cared about you, or that you were being overlooked or neglected?
2. Have you ever run away from home or were tempted to run away from home?
3. Have you ever thought of killing yourself? Have you told anyone about your thoughts?
4. Do you often compare yourself to others and to what others have?
5. What should you do if you feel like running away or doing something that you know is wrong? Who can you talk to about your problems?
6. What do you need to do to be content in life?

APPENDAGE I: THE SEARCH FOR THE PERFECT CHRISTMAS TREE

THE TALE END OF THE SERMON – CHAPTER NINE

PROVERBS 2:11, *"Discretion shall preserve thee, understanding shall keep thee:"*

PROVERBS 28:20, *"A faithful man shall abound with blessings: but he that maketh haste to be rich shall not be innocent."*

1. List the poor decisions made in search for the perfect Christmas tree.
2. How important is good decision-making in life?
3. Have you ever made any quick decisions you regretted?
4. How would you instruct someone from the Bible to know the will of God? What are the Biblical principles of good decision-making?
5. Do you have any major decisions you need to make right now? What are they?

APPENDIX J: "ALLISSA, GUESS WHO IS COMING FOR CHRISTMAS?"

THE TALE END OF THE STORY – CHAPTER TEN

ECCLESIASTES 3:1-11, *"To every thing there is a season, and a time to every purpose under the heaven: A time to be born, and a time to die; a time to plant, and a time to pluck up that which is planted; A time to kill, and a time to heal; a time to break down, and a time to build up; A time to weep, and a time to laugh; a time to mourn, and a time to dance; A time to cast away stones, and a time to gather stones together; a time to embrace, and a time to refrain from embracing; A time to get, and a time to lose; a time to keep, and a time to cast away; A time to rend, and a time to sew; a time to keep silence, and a time to speak; A time to love, and a time to hate; a time of war, and a time of peace. What profit hath he that worketh in that wherein he laboureth? I have seen the travail, which God hath given to the sons of men to be exercised in it. He hath made every thing beautiful in his time: also he hath set the world in their heart, so that no man can find out the work that God maketh from the beginning to the end."*

1. What would have been the proper steps for Joe and Will to do to make amends for shooting out the windshield of the car with the BB gun?

2. What should you do if you have a friend tempting you to do the wrong things?

3. Why was Mr. Rollins hesitant to loan the money to help the boys get home? Why did Mrs. Rollins want to loan them the money?

4. What were the major contrasts between Will's first trip to Florida with Joe and his second trip?

5. List the obvious divine appointments in the story.

APPENDIX K: I SURVIVED THE CHATTOOGA RIVER

THE TALE END OF THE STORY – CHAPTER ELEVEN

ACTS 27:9-10, *"Now when much time was spent, and when sailing was now dangerous, because the fast was now already past, Paul admonished them, [10] And said unto them, Sirs, I perceive that this voyage will be with hurt and much damage, not only of the lading and ship, but also of our lives."*

ACTS 27:14-20, *"But not long after there arose against it a tempestuous wind, called Euroclydon. And when the ship was caught, and could not bear up into the wind, we let her drive. And running under a certain island which is called Clauda, we had much work to come by the boat: Which when they had taken up, they used helps, undergirding the ship; and, fearing lest they should fall into the quicksands, strake sail, and so were driven. And we being exceedingly tossed with a tempest, the next day they lightened the ship; And the third day we cast out with our own hands the tackling of the ship. And when neither sun nor stars in many days appeared, and no small tempest lay on us, all hope that we should be saved was then taken away."*

1. Paul suffered several shipwrecks during his life. Read Acts 27. What does this account have in common with the Chattooga River adventure?
2. When should husbands listen to their wives? Are there any good or bad examples in the Bible of men who listened to the advice of their wives?
3. What would be a fun, team-building activity for missionaries to do with the church family during a mission's conference? Cite some of your own ideas.
4. List in order (#1 to #8) who you think the most endangered person was to the least endangered person in the story. Explain why.
5. Does God protect fools?
6. List three important lessons gleaned from this chapter.

APPERCEPTION L: VISION FOR THE USE OF TECHNOLOGY IN MINISTRY

THE TALE END OF THE STORY – CHAPTER TWELVE

REVELATION 13:1-3, *"And I stood upon the sand of the sea, and saw a beast rise up out of the sea, having seven heads and ten horns, and upon his horns ten crowns, and upon his heads the name of blasphemy. And the beast which I saw was like unto a leopard, and his feet were as the feet of a bear, and his mouth as the mouth of a lion: and the dragon gave him his power, and his seat, and great authority. And I saw one of his heads as it were wounded to death; and his deadly wound was healed: and all the world wondered after the beast."*
1. Can you identify who this beast is? Who is the dragon?
2. Was the beast killed? How did he come alive? Why was he worshipped?

REVELATION 13:11-16, *"And I beheld another beast coming up out of the earth; and he had two horns like a lamb, and he spake as a dragon. [12] And he exerciseth all the power of the first beast before him, and causeth the earth and them which dwell therein to worship the first beast, whose deadly wound was healed. [13] And he doeth great wonders, so that he maketh fire come down from heaven on the earth in the sight of men, [14] And deceiveth them that dwell on the earth by the means of those miracles which he had power to do in the sight of the beast; saying to them that dwell on the earth, that they should make an image to the beast, which had the wound by a sword, and did live. And he had power to give life unto the image of the beast, that the image of the beast should both speak, and cause that as many as would not worship the image of the beast should be killed. And he causeth all, both small and great, rich and poor, free and bond, to receive a mark in their right hand, or in their foreheads:"*
1. Who is this second beast? What is his relationship to the first beast? How is he different?
2. What is the image that is going to be worshipped? Potentially, how will technology be used in the worship of the image?
3. How could technology be used with the mark of the beast?

APPREHENSION M: THE MYSTERIES OF THE PARCO INN

THE TALE END OF THE STORY – CHAPTER THIRTEEN

PSALM 56:1-4, *"Be merciful unto me, O God: for man would swallow me up; he fighting daily oppresseth me. Mine enemies would daily swallow me up: for they be many that fight against me, O thou most High. What time I am afraid, I will trust in thee. In God I will praise his word, in God I have put my trust; I will not fear what flesh can do unto me."*

1. What are the battles that you are facing? Who are your enemies? Who scares you?
2. Who should you trust when you are afraid? Is there a time in the day that you are more afraid? Is there a time that would not be good for God to help you?
3. What are you afraid of the most?
4. Who are you afraid of the most?

PSALM 56:5-13, *"Every day they wrest my words: all their thoughts are against me for evil. They gather themselves together, they hide themselves, they mark my steps, when they wait for my soul. Shall they escape by iniquity? in thine anger cast down the people, O God. Thou tellest my wanderings: put thou my tears into thy bottle: are they not in thy book? When I cry unto thee, then shall mine enemies turn back: this I know; for God is for me. In God will I praise his word: in the LORD will I praise his word. In God have I put my trust: I will not be afraid what man can do unto me. Thy vows are upon me, O God: I will render praises unto thee. For thou hast delivered my soul from death: wilt not thou deliver my feet from falling, that I may walk before God in the light of the living?"*

1. What are you afraid of people saying about you? What lies have hurt you?
2. Does God see your tears? Is God for you or against you?
3. When you are fearful, what are some positive things that you can do based on Psalm 56?

APPROBATION N: THE LIFE OF A TRUE SKONGAL

THE TALE END OF THE STORY – CHAPTER FOURTEEN

THE STORY OF THE PRODIGAL SON

LUKE 15:11-24, *"And he said, A certain man had two sons: And the younger of them said to his father, Father, give me the portion of goods that falleth to me. And he divided unto them his living. And not many days after the younger son gathered all together, and took his journey into a far country, and there wasted his substance with riotous living. And when he had spent all, there arose a mighty famine in that land; and he began to be in want. And he went and joined himself to a citizen of that country; and he sent him into his fields to feed swine. And he would fain have filled his belly with the husks that the swine did eat: and no man gave unto him. And when he came to himself, he said, How many hired servants of my father's have bread enough and to spare, and I perish with hunger! I will arise and go to my father, and will say unto him, Father, I have sinned against heaven, and before thee, And am no more worthy to be called thy son: make me as one of thy hired servants. And he arose, and came to his father. But when he was yet a great way off, his father saw him, and had compassion, and ran, and fell on his neck, and kissed him. And the son said unto him, Father, I have sinned against heaven, and in thy sight, and am no more worthy to be called thy son. But the father said to his servants, Bring forth the best robe, and put it on him; and put a ring on his hand, and shoes on his feet: And bring hither the fatted calf, and kill it; and let us eat, and be merry: For this my son was dead, and is alive again; he was lost, and is found. And they began to be merry."*

1. In which ways was Will like the prodigal son? In which ways are you like the prodigal son?

2. How many times can you recall in your life someone trying to point you to God? Who has had the greatest influence shaping your spiritual life?

3. Do you need to be baptized to go to heaven? Does God have an approved list of churches that He checks to see if you are a member before He lets you into heaven?

4. Can a person ever do enough good works and religious things to demand God to let him into His heaven? How is one truly saved?